*Reframing Christian Education
for a Global Generation*

HORIZONS IN RELIGIOUS EDUCATION is a book series sponsored by the Religious Education Association: An Association of Professors, Practitioners, and Researchers in Religious Education. It was established to promote new scholarship and exploration in the academic field of Religious Education. The series will include both seasoned educators and newer scholars and practitioners just establishing their academic writing careers.

Books in this series reflect religious and cultural diversity, educational practice, living faith, and the common good of all people. They are chosen on the basis of their contributions to the vitality of religious education around the globe. Writers in this series hold deep commitments to their own faith traditions, yet their work sets forth claims that might also serve other religious communities, strengthen academic insight, and connect the pedagogies of religious education to the best scholarship of numerous cognate fields.

The posture of the Religious Education Association has always been ecumenical and multi-religious, attuned to global contexts, and committed to affecting public life. These values are grounded in the very institutions, congregations, and communities that transmit religious faith. The association draws upon the interdisciplinary richness of religious education connecting theological, spiritual, religious, social science and cultural research and wisdom. Horizons of Religious Education aims to heighten understanding and appreciation of the depth of scholarship resident within the discipline of religious education, as well as the ways it impacts our common life in a fragile world. Without a doubt, we are inspired by the wonder of teaching and the awe that must be taught.

Reframing Christian Education for a Global Generation

Heesung Hwang

Foreword by Hosffman Ospino, Mai-Anh Le Tran, Elizabeth Conde-Frazier, and Jack L. Seymour

◆PICKWICK *Publications* • Eugene, Oregon

REFRAMING CHRISTIAN EDUCATION FOR A GLOBAL GENERATION

Horizons in Religious Education

Copyright © 2024 Heesung Hwang. All rights reserved. Except for brief quotations in critical publications or reviews, no part of this book may be reproduced in any manner without prior written permission from the publisher. Write: Permissions, Wipf and Stock Publishers, 199 W. 8th Ave., Suite 3, Eugene, OR 97401.

Pickwick Publications
An Imprint of Wipf and Stock Publishers
199 W. 8th Ave., Suite 3
Eugene, OR 97401

www.wipfandstock.com

PAPERBACK ISBN: 979-8-3852-1537-9
HARDCOVER ISBN: 979-8-3852-1538-6
EBOOK ISBN: 979-8-3852-1539-3

Cataloguing-in-Publication data:

Names: Hwang, Heesung, author. | Ospino, Hosffman, foreword. | Tran, Mai-Anh Le, foreword. | Conde-Frazier, Elizabeth, foreword. | Seymour, Jack L., foreword.

Title: Reframing Christian education for a global generation / Heesung Hwang ; foreword by Hosffman Ospino, Mai-Anh Le Tran, Elizabeth Conde-Frazier, and Jack L. Seymour.

Description: Eugene, OR : Pickwick Publications, 2024 | Series: Horizons in Religious Education | Includes bibliographical references.

Identifiers: ISBN 979-8-3852-1537-9 (paperback) | ISBN 979-8-3852-1538-6 (hardcover) | ISBN 979-8-3852-1539-3 (ebook)

Subjects: LCSH: Christian education. | Education and globalization.

Classification: LC383 .H83 2024 (paperback) | LC383 .H83 (ebook)

09/19/24

Scripture quotations are from the Common English Bible®, CEB® Copyright © 2010, 2011 by Common English Bible.™ Used by permission. All rights reserved worldwide.

In honor of all the children and families I encountered on my journey—
thank you for sharing your courage, tears, love, and hope with me.

CONTENTS

List of Figures | ix
Editorial Review Board | xi
Foreword by Hosffman Ospino, Mai-Anh Le Tran, Elizabeth Conde-Frazier, and Jack L. Seymour | xiii
Acknowledgments | xvii
Introduction | xix

Chapter 1: Here Comes the New Generation: Shin Yi Se | 1
Chapter 2: "So Korean" Wherever You Are | 20
Chapter 3: Becoming Like Children | 42
Chapter 4: How Do They Grow Up? | 53
Chapter 5: Come Play in Our Madang | 67
Chapter 6: Signs of Madang, the Redemptive Community | 81

Conclusion | 91
Bibliography | 97

LIST OF FIGURES

Figure 1: Application of the triple-heritage model of Christian education to Korean American churches | xxv

Figure 2: Madang as a liberating space for a house of being | xxvi

Figure 3: Timeline of events and generations in the 21st century in the US | 3

Figure 4: A breakdown of the child population in the US by race, 2019 | 8

Figure 5: Percentages of immigrants by race and projections | 10

Figure 6: Ages of US Koreans in 2019, by percent of Korean population | 12

Figure 7: Scaffolding for a child's house of being | 56

Figure 8: Bronfenbrenner's bioecological model of human development, modified | 58

Figure 9: Madang as a liberating playground for a house of being | 73

HORIZONS in RELIGIOUS EDUCATION— EDITORIAL REVIEW BOARD

Editorial Review Board
—Jack L. Seymour (co-editor), Garrett-Evangelical Theological Seminary

—Hosffman Ospino (co-editor), Boston College

—Mai-Anh Le Tran (co-editor), Garrett-Evangelical Theological Seminary

Class of 2021
—Dean G. Blevins, Nazarene Theological Seminary

—N. Lynne Westfield, The Wabash Center for Teaching and Learning in Religion and Theology

—Maureen O'Brien, Duquesne University

Class of 2022
—Elizabeth Conde-Frazier, Association for Hispanic Theological Education

—Sheryl Kujawa-Holbrook, Claremont School of Theology

—Boyung Lee, Iliff School of Theology

EDITORIAL REVIEW BOARD

Class of 2023

—Deborah Court, Bar Ilan University

—Harold Horell, Fordham University

—Katherine Turpin, Iliff School of Theology

FOREWORD

MILLIONS OF YOUNG PEOPLE throughout the world are growing up as children of the diaspora. Affected by contemporary globalization forces, mass migration movements, political and climate displacement, their families have relocated geographically and culturally, searching for new opportunities or simply fleeing from adversities that prevent them from reaching their full potential.

These young people are growing up in between worlds. On the one hand, the world that their parents try to recreate at home, with traditions, rituals and practices that keep them connected to faraway homelands, building on memories and relationships that fade in time, often speaking languages that are different from that of their neighbors. On the other hand, the world where they currently live, as citizens of societies that do not always recognize them as such; negotiating values and worldviews that are often dissonant when compared to what they experience at home. Both worlds are simultaneously theirs and not. Their lives unfold in a constant process of negotiating identities and commitments, including what it means to be a person of faith in pluralistic and increasingly secularized societies.

Rev. Dr. Heesung Hwang gifts the *Horizons in Religious Education* series with a wonderful book that looks closely at the cultural and religious experience of this young population. *Reframing Christian Education for a Global Generation* focuses on the particular experience of Korean American second—or third—generation children of recent diasporic (im)migrants children in Protestant Christian communities in the United States. As such, the book is a case study that promises to resonate with the realities of many other young Christians and young people discerning their cultural and religious identity in other racial/ethnic communities and faith traditions.

FOREWORD

These second-generation children of immigrants, sometimes called "third culture kids," challenge religious educators not only to revisit the methodological and curricular assumptions that shape our faith formation efforts, but also to engage these young people in the process of making sense of religion in their hybrid lives. Their multiple cultural belonging, their common ability to speak several languages, the strong influence of adult immigrants at home, and the tensions associated with an existence "in-between" matter significantly as we imagine religious education experiences with them. Dr. Hwang rightly reminds us that the complexity of being second generation is akin to being a "new humanity."

The commitment to thinking and developing fresher approaches for religious education with second-generation young people is close to Dr. Hwang's life project. As a minister and a theologian, she has long journeyed with many Korean American young people and their families. She has heard their stories. She knows the needs and hopes of her community. The experience of these young people served as a resource for the research that grounded her doctoral dissertation and now this book. Here we encounter a fine example of scholarship born from ministerial and religious educational praxis, thus reclaiming a major source of wisdom for the religious educators in the academy.

Drawing from the best of the Korean cultural tradition, Dr. Hwang introduces a vision for religious education inspired in the traditional Korean architectural concept of *madang*. The term translates into English as "courtyard." It is that open space in many traditional Korean homes, and in the homes of several other cultures, where the family gathers to spend time together, eat, play, hear stories, engage in conversation, and build relationships. Dr. Hwang invites faith communities to become *madangs*, open spaces where religious education happens as the natural result of communal interaction, where all members of the community are engaged and their contributions are valued in their own right. Young and old, citizen and immigrant, family and friends all together in an effort to ensure the continuity of the faith as lived and practiced from one generation to the next. In the *madang*, religious education occurs as an experience where everyone enters, explores, plays and blesses.

There is no doubt that this book will generate important conversations and we want to invite you to read it and discuss it with other faith educators. Religious education in faith communities that organize themselves as *madangs* are more likely to be generative spaces for second and subsequent generations of multi or intercultural young people to share their hopes, questions and concerns. These are redemptive communities that connect people, culture, faith and heritage, says Dr. Hwang. Such are the faith communities that religious educators need to foster today in order to accompany young people who are making meaning and becoming creators of new cultures, new identities, and new cultural and religious expressions in the church and wider society today.

— HOSFFMAN OSPINO, Boston College, Boston, Massachusetts. Co-chair, *HORIZONS* Editorial Board

— MAI-ANH LE TRAN, Garrett-Evangelical Theological Seminary, Evanston, Illinois, U.S.A. Co-chair, *HORIZONS* Editorial Board

— ELIZABETH CONDE-FRAZIER, Association for Hispanic Theological Education (AETH) Orlando, Florida, U.S.A. Co-chair, *HORIZONS* Editorial Board

— JACK L. SEYMOUR, Professor Emeritus, Garrett-Evangelical Theological Seminary, Evanston, Illinois. Co-chair, *HORIZONS* Editorial Board

ACKNOWLEDGMENTS

STANDING ON A BEACH and looking out at the horizon has always given me a sense of peace and wonder. As I walked along a small stream, observing its sounds and the flow of life in it, I reached the vast sea and stood in awe of the magnificent intersection of life and time. The huge waves reminded me that the little brook was never small, and that it had never been trivial. There is phenomenal and divine potential in every delicate flow. In this sense, writing this book was such a delightful journey. My commitment to faith communities and love for children led me to a PhD program, in which I continued to study Christian education and the role of the church in our rapidly changing society. All the steps were pleasant and meaningful, like walking along a stream and finally reaching the ocean. I hope you also enjoy your journey of reading this as if you are walking alongside your own stream. And I hope you encounter your own ocean at the end.

The content of this book was derived from my PhD dissertation, so I would like to extend my sincere thanks to the congregations that have nurtured my dissertation work and all the interviewees and children I have encountered. You are the reason for my ministry and research.

I have been supported by many people throughout my research journey. I'm especially grateful to Jack L. Seymour and Boyung Lee for carefully reviewing my manuscript and giving me endless guidance and encouragement throughout the publishing process. To Virginia Lee, Margaret Ann Crain, and Mai-Anh Le Tran, thank you for believing in my potential and my research. And a special thanks to my copyeditor, Vicki Wiltse. This book would not have been possible to complete without your thorough review and editing. It was a blessing for me to work with you. Many thanks to my immediate and extended family members and to my dearest friends,

Acknowledgments

WooJiMan, Mikang, and the Huhs, for the love and prayers you have given me throughout the years.

    Lastly, I would like to thank my husband, Dooyong Kang, for all the love, encouragement, and support he has given me. It is because of you, Dooyong, that I am able to write and do research. Without you, I wouldn't be where I am today. Thank you, and I love you.

INTRODUCTION

CAUGHT UP IN THE RAPIDS: CONTEMPORARY KOREAN AMERICAN CHURCHES AND THE PANDEMIC

Entering 2020, everyone was suddenly caught up in the rapids of social change. Until then, we had been paddling in relatively manageable water; then the threat of the coronavirus changed our lives at an unpredictable pace and magnitude. To put it more precisely, the pandemic accelerated the changes that had been taking place, and revealed many sociocultural problems that had been latent. We must now talk about this crisis and the hope for humanity, the economic impact of the pandemic, and the issues of racism and violence. Of course, these are not new issues that have only emerged recently. These problems have been around in US society for a long time, and sometimes they seem to be lessening. However, they became more intensely visible with the sudden coronavirus crisis. The pandemic heightened social anxiety and created a sense of crisis. Anti-Asian sentiments and hate crimes spread and continued into 2021.[1] In particular, the Atlanta spa shootings, which happened on March 16, 2021, revealed the realities of the lives of Asian women who have been in the land of the United States for hundreds of years but are still treated as exotic foreigners.[2] Now, our children are asking us questions: Is there hope for the world we will live

---

1. L. Zhou, "History of Anti-Asian Hate"; Blanding and Solomon, "Coronavirus Is Fueling Fear"; Chavez, "Asian Americans Reported Being Targeted."

2. Helsel and Elbaum, "8 Dead in Atlanta-Area Shootings"; G. J. Kim, *Embracing the Other*, 13, 17.

in? Is there hope in our church? Is there an alternative to the church and religious education as we now know it?

This book was written while the US was going through a torrent of social change. It is the result of a decade of thinking about what Christian religious education should do for future generations. My research is not merely a story about (or for) a particular ethnic group, but a look at a meaningful approach to church for everyone and for all who have not given up hope in religious education. By looking at Korean immigrant churches and their children's education ministries, which have not been discussed much before, this book will provide a breakthrough for religious education in the twenty-first and twenty-second centuries in the United States.

SHIN YI SE: EMERGING NEW SECOND-GENERATION IMMIGRANT CHILDREN

For this research study, the group I was primarily interested in was Korean American children who were five to eleven years old in 2020 and their families. Specifically, I was concerned with children who are classified (according to the existing definition) as 1.5- or second-generation immigrant children, meaning their parents were Korean immigrants who predominantly used the Korean language and followed Korean culture.[3] However, if we examine the cultural and social backgrounds of immigrant families more carefully, the definition becomes more complex. As the history of immigration continues and Asian American studies becomes a more active field, the terms for and ways of discussing second-generation Asian Americans are a subject being addressed by many scholars. So, to be more precise, the generation I have researched for this project is the generation following those examined in previous studies.

In their collaborative book, *Sustaining Faith Traditions*, Russell Jeung, Carolyn Chen, and Jerry Park note, "With the passage of the 1965 Immigrant Act and the 1990 Immigration Act, newcomers from Latin America and Asia have significantly changed the racial make-up of the United

---

3. In general, "The second generation is defined as those who are born and raised in the United States with at least one immigrant parent. 1.5 generation is defined as those who are not born in the United States but are raised and schooled primarily in the United States. The first generation is defined as those who were born and raised largely in Korea." Kim and Kim, "Korean American Christians' Communities," 190n1.

States."[4] In their analysis and according to their definition, the *new second generation* of Latinos and Asian Americans consists of the children of immigrants who arrived in the US as a result of changes in US immigration policy beginning in 1965. Many research projects have focused on the cultural conflicts between first- and second-generation Asian Americans and the role of Asian American communities in navigating those conflicts.[5] A need remains for more research on such topics as generations of Asian Americans continue to flourish in between two different cultural worlds, each generation striving to claim its own voice in the twenty-first century.[6]

However, it should be noted that the experiences of Asian Americans in the new second generation whose parents came as a result of the 1965 Immigrant Act have been very different from those whose parents came after the Immigration Act of 1990. Although the focus of my research was also "second-generation" immigrants, their cultural manifestations vary from those of the "new second generation." Specifically, my research interest was the lives of those second-generation immigrants who were the children of at least one Korean immigrant parent who was categorized as Gen X or as an early Millennial.[7] This second generation, which has enjoyed K-pop (such as Psy's "Gangnam Style" and BTS's and Black Pink's chart-topping hit songs) and a Korean cultural wave as the new norm globally, is different. This generation, growing up with high technology and high mobility, is different. The social and economic experiences of this generation are different from those of past generations. Therefore, I will call these second-generation children Shin Yi Se to distinguish them from second-generation or new-second-generation immigrant Americans.[8]

In Korean, the term shin in ryu (신인류; 新人類), meaning "new humanity" or "new species," refers to a new generation that has emerged as a result of rapid sociocultural changes. The term *shin in ryu* is not only given to a specific generation. It is also a general term that refers to the advent of a new era. Yi se is a word commonly used when speaking of the second

4. Jeung, Chen, and Park, "Identities of the New Second Generation," 4.
5. Ty, *Asianfail*, 18.
6. Ty, *Asianfail*, 7; Han and Hsu, *Asian American X*, 5–7.
7. *Generation X* refers to those who were born between 1965 and 1979. Following Gen X, *Millennials* refers to those who were born between 1980 and 1994. New second generation Koreans generally belong to Gen X or the Millennials.
8. The terms *Asian American* and *Korean American* are used interchangeably in this study. Although my theoretical exploration is based on Asian American studies in general, my interpretations focus mainly on Korean Americans.

generation in Korean. Hence, *Shin Yi Se* literally means "the new second generation"; it is a compound of "new humanity" and "second generation," and it is designed to refer to the second generation of immigrants growing up during the pandemic in the twenty-first century. I have proposed the new name *Shin Yi Se* as an alternative to *new second generation* in order to go beyond the limitations of immigrant and generational research conducted so far. This term will help scholars pay attention to changes in the characteristics and culture of current second-generation children.

However, some sociocultural phenomena continue across generations. One example is racialized social norms. Jeung, Chen, and Park point out that the new second generation shares with previous generations the experience of being considered and treated as foreigners by the majority group.[9] Significantly, racial stereotypes—whether they are good or bad—become internalized and dwell in people's minds so that they assume these stereotypes are true. As Richard Slotkin, a historian and cultural critic, states, "A people unaware of its myths is likely to continue living by them, though the world around that people may change and demand changes in their psychology, their worldview, their ethics, and their institutions."[10] This phenomenon continues to this day without any sign of disappearing or changing.[11] To children who are at the stage of forming their faith and identity, racial stereotypes and social pressures add more layers of challenge to overcome.

Over the last fifteen years, while serving Korean American churches in various settings and teaching in a theological seminary, I have witnessed the challenges the rising generation is going through in their families and society. Living in between cultures with two different languages, this rising generation is constantly struggling with cultural conflicts and identity formation. At home, they deal with different cultural traditions and ways of communication with their parents. At school and in society, they deal with racism and marginalization.[12]

Korean church education has, in general, rarely taught individuals how to live and communicate with others across races, cultures, and religions.

9. Jeung, Chen, and Park, "Identities of the New Second Generation," 7.

10. Slotkin, *Regeneration through Violence*, 4–5; Lisa Park, "Significance of the Model Minority Myth," 505.

11. S. J. Lee, *Unraveling the "Model Minority" Stereotype*, 11.

12. Sharon Kim and Rebecca Y. Kim illuminate how second-generation Korean Americans have similar struggles and issues. See Kim and Kim, "Korean American Christians' Communities," 180–181.

It predominately teaches children not to worry overtly about racial issues or other religious problems that the broader society faces; rather, it teaches children to focus more on personal or familial values, personal salvation, and social success. Korean churches are pouring Korean heritage, language, and faith into children with the hope and belief that such rigorous depositing will eventually preserve their faith and that their children, growing up in this foreign land, will succeed in mainstream American society. Here, I feel a sense of crisis and cognitive dissonance as children encounter this "null curriculum" behind the meanings and values Korean immigrant churches explicitly present.[13]

In addition, throughout my ethnographic interviews with Korean American young adults, I could sense the internalized racism of several respondents and their desire to succeed in mainstream American society. According to Nazli Kibria, "Fueled by the very fact of their racialized marginality, Asian Americans may ironically affirm the stereotype of themselves as a model minority in an effort to ease their own path of integration into American society."[14] Jennifer C. Ng, Sharon S. Lee and Yoon K. Pak, in their article "Contesting the Model Minority and Perpetual Foreigner Stereotypes," argue that model minority stereotypes are not only externally given but also internally strengthened to work against Asian Americans. They add that this is particularly true "for second-generation Asians with immigrant parents."[15]

What can faith communities, even those that are not ethnic-minoritized congregations, do for the Shin Yi Se children, armed with the latest technology and living in a multi-ethnic, multicultural, multi-religious society? Is it best to just teach the Word itself without contextualizing it, to tell them to believe it without question? Is it best to bless them to be like Joseph, Daniel, or Esther, to be faithful and successful leaders in this foreign (but not foreign) land?

In this book, I analyze the current issues and challenges facing the Shin Yi Se and the practices of faith communities for children and their families who live in this era of rapid social change and globalization along with constant struggles in the midst of faith and racial stereotypes. It is not the work of an individual alone to figure out his or her own voice and purpose in life. Rather, education is the shared responsibility of parents and

---

13. Harris, *Fashion Me a People*, 69.
14. Kibria, *Becoming Asian American*, 206.
15. Ng, Lee, and Pak, "Contesting Stereotypes," 31.

community as well as oneself, so one can navigate through the meanings of one's own life and grow up as an integrated human being.

THEORETICAL FRAMEWORKS FOR THE MADANG APPROACH

This book will explore sociocultural and political influences on second-generation Korean American children and youth that form the characteristics of Generation Z and Generation Alpha, theories of child development and faith development, theologies of childhood, Asian American practical theology, and religious education in a globalizing society. Through these foundational categories, and through ethnographic research in Korean immigrant congregations, I will develop a way to communicate more effectively with Shin Yi Se children and their families. My discussion of each of these categories is based on Yolanda Smith's triple-heritage model and Paulo Freire's pedagogy of the oppressed.

In her book *Reclaiming the Spirituals*, Smith identifies three major factors that influence the spiritual formation of African American adolescents: African heritage, African American heritage, and Christian heritage. These factors form a "triple-heritage model" for the African American church. Each component works distinctively and cooperatively in interaction with the other components in an African American youth's life.[16] "The central point of intersection is where the spirituals draw the three components together and where the reflection upon the educational process begins."[17] This triple-heritage model of Christian education, which was designed for a particular racial group (African Americans), offers great insight into and new possibilities for Korean American Christian education. With a replacement of one of the three components—"African heritage" with "Korean heritage"—and the deletion of "African" in the second component, the intersection of the three heritages reflects a practice that approaches Korean American children on the basis of a collaborative understanding and relationship among the three categories (see figure 1). While minor variations in their choice of terms existed—such as "best friends," "family," and "Korean church community"—the people I interviewed for this study expressed their yearning for creating meaningful relationships in faith as a way of preserving the three heritages. Considering the redemptive ministry

---

16. Y. Smith, *Reclaiming the Spirituals*, 12–14.
17. Y. Smith, *Reclaiming the Spirituals*, 13.

of Jesus, in which Jesus responded to people's needs in their own locations, Korean immigrant churches and their education ministries should deal with Korean immigrants' lives and children's education issues in more proactive, liberating, and comprehensive ways.

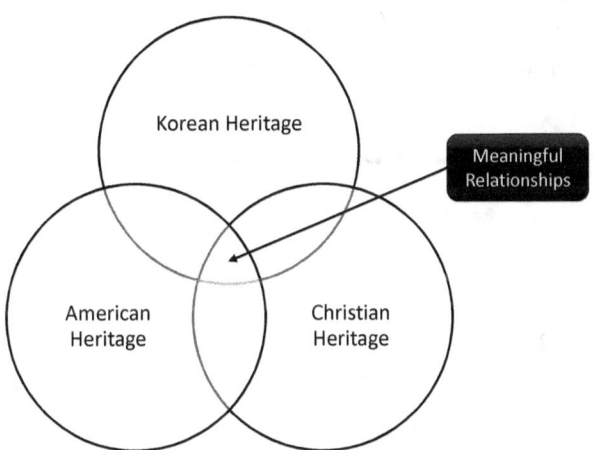

Figure 1. Application of the triple-heritage model of Christian education to Korean American churches

It is important to create safe and open spaces in which Shin Yi Se immigrant children can navigate various possibilities for developing their faith and creating their own identities beyond any racial stereotypes.[18] Therefore, I propose the *Madang* approach for these children and their faith communities in order to open up spaces for constructive social interactions, so that children and adults can be nurtured into becoming integrated, creative human beings who are not confused or divided between different cultures and traditions. In Korean architecture, a *madang*, which is called a courtyard in a Western house, is an open, flat space found in every traditional Korean home that is used for individual activities, for a family's projects, or for communal events. Almost half of Koreans in modern society live in apartments, so the presence of individual houses and madangs has become less common than it used to be. Its conceptual use continues, however, when people refer to spaces shared by community members as madangs, even when they are not privately owned.[19] The spirit of madang still applies to

18. S. Kim, *Faith of Our Own*, 162; hooks, *Teaching to Transgress*, 185–86.
19. Yoo, "아파트에서 살면서도 '집집마다 앞마당' 누리며 살 수 있다면."

Introduction

apartment complexes and public spaces and has expanded to virtual spaces. It is on the basis of such a concept and value that I dig deep to study community sharing and the communal growth of life and narratives. In that regard, I argue that religious education in faith communities should aim to offer a liberating space—Madang —for the Shin Yi Se, a space where children are encouraged to raise questions of their teachers and to learn the skills to engage the wisdom of their community and where teachers can freely discuss faith, texts, and the realities of life with young students.[20]

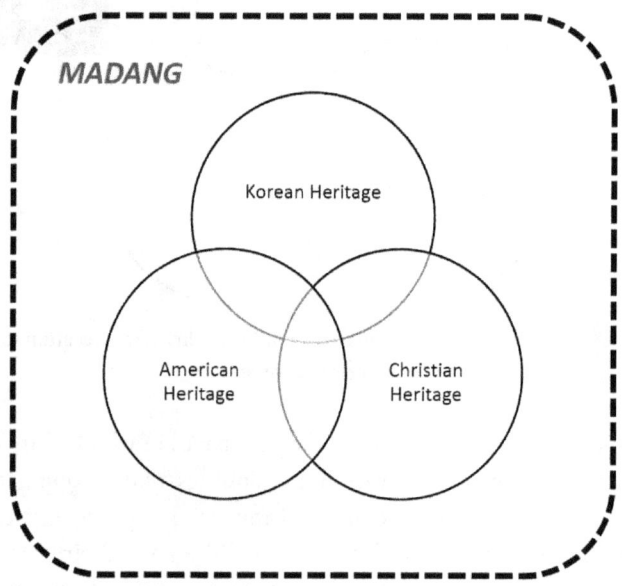

Figure 2. Madang as a liberating space for a house of being

A Madang can be a new type of playground for the emerging generation, as well as for immigrant children. I believe it is a way to heal, recharge, and strengthen the bonds of individuals and families in a congregation—as well as in wider social circles—and a way to practice transformative and liberating power in our little corner of the world. I hope my research will contribute to a better and more useful understanding of immigrants' identity formation and ministry to them by presenting the Madang approach as a new ecclesiology for the twenty-first century. The Madang approach

20. Freire, *Pedagogy of the Oppressed*, 83–86.

will also remind us Christians that it is not an entirely new way but has roots in our long tradition of fellowship and small group movements. Thus, we can renew our hope for the church in the twenty-first century and for the possibility of abundant life together for Gen Z, Gen Alpha, and those generations that follow.

Chapter 1

HERE COMES THE NEW GENERATION: SHIN YI SE

SOO JEONG

I was shopping to buy a birthday gift. One of the young workers in the store, who looked like a Latina, came to me and asked, "Are you Korean?" I was surprised. The question I had often received for years was whether I was Chinese. "Yes, I'm Korean," I said. With my reply, she was so excited that she shared her story. She said, "My best friends at school are Korean and I listen to Korean Pop music. . . . I recently met a Korean Pop star who came to the shopping mall. Do you know so and so?" I barely knew any K-pop groups, much less any of the individuals in each group of nine to thirteen members, but this girl knew the names of their songs and members. Then she rolled up her sleeve and showed me her left arm. On her arm was a tattoo that said 수정 (*Soo Jeong*). Her tattoo was written in Korean characters, and she said it was her Korean name.

After having a short conversation with this young woman about her knowledge of Korean culture and K-pop stars, I came out of the store with a purchase and feeling somewhat strange. Her kindness and her positive attitude toward Korean culture were remarkable, and the Korean tattoo was more so. In Korea, I would see tattoos with all kinds of English letters and images. In the United States, I never imagined a day when a young Hispanic girl would be carrying a Korean tattoo and talking about K-pop.

OVERALL PICTURE OF THE LIFE OF THIS GENERATION

As I indicated in the introduction, my target research group was second-generation immigrant children who were aged five to eleven years old at the time of the study, making them part of Gen Z or Gen Alpha. Culturally, their parents were in the category of Gen X or early Millennials. Although generational characteristics presented in cultural studies do not exactly fit immigrant families, sociocultural analyses on younger generations provide helpful insights for understanding children in the twenty-first century. And while ethnic studies also provide great analyses of the second generation of Asian Americans, they do not provide a comprehensive interpretation of the intersectionality of culture, society, and technology in the US.

Figure 3 presents a glimpse of the world of my research subjects, Shin Yi Se Korean American children and their families. It was created to portray the intersectionality of the Shin Yi Se in a globalizing society in the first two decades of the twenty-first century. The years in black stand for the lives of those in Generation Z, and the years in light gray indicate the years of Generation Alpha. The gray highlight underneath the years, which starts in 2007 and continues to the present, indicates my target research group. My target research group, therefore, includes both young Gen Zers and early Gen Alphas. In addition to organizing the two generations, I added major events during their lifespans and coded them by three major influence markers. The Influence Marker A indicates the development of major communication technologies and social media platforms. The Influence Marker B shows major social events in the United States. The Influence Marker C represents the global influence of Korean culture.

Year	2001	2002	2003	2004	2005	2006
A	Wikipedia, iPod			Google, Facebook	YouTube, Twitter	
B	9/11 Terrorist Attack, New York					Hurricane Katrina in New Orleans
C						
Year	2007	2008	2009	2010	2011	2012
A	Apple iPhone 1st Gen.		TED Talks, WhatsApp	Instagram, iPad 1st Gen.	Snapchat	
B	Virginia Tech Mass Shooting	U.S. Economy Collapses	Obama's Presidency			Sandy Hook ES Mass Shooting
C		"Hallyu 2.0" Global Recognition of New Korean Wave				Psy, "Gangnam Style" Worldwide Hit
Year	2013	2014	2015	2016	2017	2018
A	ZOOM	Smart iWatch 1st Gen.		TikTok	iPhone X AI Robots	
B	Black Lives Matter Movement		Same-sex Marriage Legalized	Orlando Gay Bar Mass Shooting	Trump's Presidency; #Metoo Movement; Immigration Restriction Policy; Las Vegas, Texas, NY Mass Shootings	Over 300 Mass Shootings; Family Separation at the US-Mexico border
C					BTS Becomes the First K-Pop Group to Perform at an American Music Award Show	
Year	2019	2020	2021	2022	\multicolumn{2}{l}{My Target Research Group}
A	Samsung Galaxy Fold 1st Gen.		Meta Platforms	ChatGPT	Influence Markers:	
B	Over 400 Mass Shootings	COVID-19 Pandemic; 611 Mass Shootings	COVID-19 Pandemic; Biden's Presidency; 692 Mass Shootings	COVID-19 Pandemic; 647 Mass Shootings	A. Development of technology, search engines, & social media platforms B. Major social events in the U.S. C. Korea-related cultural influence	
C	The Korean Movie, Parasite, Worldwide Hit	BTS #1 in Billboard HOT 100				

Figure 3. Timeline of events and generations in the 21st century in the US[1]

1. The term *Hallyu 2.0* indicates the New Korean Wave thriving through social media, such as YouTube, Instagram, Viki, and DramaFever, from 2008 to the present. Sources for the figure: Banda, "Events that Shaped the US"; Vmiller373, "2000-2010 Major Events"; Barnicoat and Woolf, "Decade Timeline"; "2000-2009 Timeline Contents"; "2010-2019 Timeline Contents"; Corey, "2017 Year in Review"; Ho, "*Crazy Rich Asians*"; Chiu, "All-Asian Cast"; Jin, *New Korean Wave*, 123-51; Lynch, "BTS"; Sergent, "Mass Shootings During 2020."

In the last twenty years, we have experienced more rapid changes than we have ever experienced before. Such changes have been based on incredibly rapidly developing technologies. The emergence of smartphones in 2007 has especially changed the way we communicate and live. It is noteworthy that Korean culture has been recognized globally since the early 2010s. Dal Young Jin notes, "[In] recent years, Korea has become the top non-Western country that meaningfully exports almost all of its cultural forms, such as television programs, film, popular music, animation, and digital technologies, including online gaming and smartphones (not only as technology but also as culture) to both Western and non-Western countries."[2] The K-pop culture is changing the perception of Korea and its diaspora. Thanks to the development of technology and social network systems, PSY's "Gangnam Style" achieved over a billion views on YouTube worldwide in 2012—the year the song was released—making it "the first video in the history of the Internet to reach and surpass one billion views."[3] In 2020, BTS and Black Pink were the trend-leading K-pop groups in the world.[4] The younger generations in general, and second-generation Korean American children more specifically, are approaching Korean culture more easily and positively. The advancements in technology give children various opportunities to acquire information by themselves and to create a culture of their own. Children of this new era live locally but communicate with others and transform one another globally.

Meanwhile, people in the United States are experiencing extreme anxiety about life and social conflicts due to increasing terrorism and mass shootings. What I found shocking while doing this research was the increasing incidents of gun violence. In the single year of 2019, there were 417 mass shootings in the US. In 2020, 611 mass shootings were reported, and unfortunately, the trend persists.[5] There have been more incidents of mass shootings and gun violence ever since. Here, *mass shooting* means three or more people were killed with a gun in a short span of time. Such repetitive violence creates a culture of fear and anger.[6]

---

2. Jin, *New Korean Wave*, 123–51.
3. Gruger, "'Gangnam Style' Hits 1 Billion Views."
4. Aderoju, "Twitter's Most Popular Musical Act!"
5. Sergent, "Mass Shootings During 2020"; Alfonseca, "More Mass Shootings than Days in 2023."
6. Silverstein, "More Mass Shootings"; Elmore, *Generation Z Unfiltered*, 38–39.

From the standpoint of a scholar of ethnic minorities and from a humanitarian point of view, the Trump administration's immigration policy (which raises the question of racial segregation), including the family separations at the border between the US and Mexico, has been deeply concerning.[7] Meanwhile, people have stepped forward to make their communities more just: the Black Lives Matter movement responded to racial discrimination, same-sex marriage was legalized, and different religious interpretations of humanity arose accordingly. In terms of Asian Americans, the successes of the movies *Parasite* (2019) and *Minari* (2020) were celebrated for enhancing the visibility of stereotypes of Asian Americans and for breaking them.[8] Various interpretations and exclusions are always inevitable social phenomena. Yet, as despair and hope coexist, Christian churches have an important task to teach children how to live faithfully and thrive in an anxious and violent world.

Shin Yi Se: Generation Z and Generation Alpha

As of 2021, the population of Generation Z was about 68.6 million, which makes up around 20.7 percent of the total US population.[9] There are different definitions of the boundaries of Gen Z, but, in general, the term refers to those who were born between 1997 and 2010. In his book *Meet Generation Z: Understanding and Reaching the New Post-Christian World*, James E. White, pastor of a multi-campus church in North Carolina, defines Gen Z as those who are living in "a post-9/11 world. They are experiencing radical changes in technology and understandings of family, sexuality, and gender. They live in multigenerational households, and the fastest-growing demographic within their age group is multiracial."[10]

White has determined that the major characteristics of Gen Zers are that they are sensitive about financial security and want to find new alternatives to the existing socioeconomic order; they are always connected to the internet; and they think social media is the most important means of communication and education.[11] In addition, they have a larger number

---

7. Hegarty, "Children Separated from Families"; Barajas, "Trump's Family Separation Policy"; Rodriguez and McDede, "Asian Americans More Stressed."
8. Serjeant, "Year After 'Parasite,' 'Minari.'"
9. Duffin, "U.S. Population by Generation 2021."
10. J. E. White, *Meet Generation Z*, 39.
11. J. E. White, *Meet Generation Z*, 38–45.

of multiracial marriages and LGBTQIA+ individuals than previous generations.[12] Gen Z is also referred to as the first post-Christian generation.[13] According to White, along with the decline of mainline denominations, the young adult generations—Gen X and Millennials—have not been as involved in religious practices as previous generations, and the so-called nones and dones have increased accordingly. Coming from Gen X and Millennial parents, Gen Z is the first generation in history to be born in a post-Christian culture. White thus claims that "the nones are no longer the second largest religious group in the United States; they are the largest."[14]

Yet, what White thinks of as a religious crisis (the crisis of the existence of the church), I think of as an opportunity for the transformation of the church and the world. In that sense, for me, Gen Z is the first generation to embody the possibilities of overthrowing existing ways of thinking and moving beyond them. It is noteworthy that the role and position of the church in Korean immigrant society is still important. Korean immigrant churches, which continue to serve as important community service and cultural centers for immigrants and their children, are still at the center of many immigrants' lives, despite the overall aging and decline of the immigrant community.

We should also pay attention to the generation after Gen Z: Generation Alpha. This newest demographic cohort refers to people born after 2010. According to Mark McCrindle, a social researcher and demographer who is leading the discussion on Generation Alpha, "Alpha kids will grow up with iPads in hand, never live without a smartphone, and have the ability to transfer a thought online in seconds. These massive technological changes, among others, make Generation Alpha the most transformative generation ever."[15] As children of Millennials, Gen Alphas are also characterized by experience with integrated technology and mobility.[16]

Gen Z and Gen Alpha are the two generations to which I am paying attention. It is urgent for churches to prepare for the transformation of existing church traditions, worship, and technology in order to prepare for the cultures of these younger generations and their children. Gen Alphas and some of the Gen Zers are now children and youth, but soon they will

12. J. E. White, *Meet Generation Z*, 45–48.
13. J. E. White, *Meet Generation Z*, 49.
14. J. E. White, *Meet Generation Z*, 22.
15. Sterbenz, "After Generation Z."
16. Berkowitz, "Alpha Generation."

become young adults and young parents of children of future generations. They are our present and the imminent future. They are not just digital natives, or the largest part of the population, but also a generation that will change America's colors, culture, and religious paths.

Colorful: A Rapid Demographic Transformation

Robert P. Jones, the CEO of the Public Religion Research Institute, in his book *The End of White Christian America*, argues that the United States will no longer be a white-centered nation by 2050.[17] He writes, "When Obama was reelected in 2012, population experts forecasted that by 2060 whites will see their numbers decline for the first time in American history, while the number of people who identify as multiracial will nearly triple and the number of Hispanics and Asians will more than double."[18] His analysis is quite right. However, this is not the future that will happen after 2050, but the reality of the current population of children. According to data from Kids Count Data Center, the ratio of non-Hispanic white minors to the total child population has decreased from 55 percent to 49 percent over the past decade, while the proportion of children of color has increased to 51 percent of the total.[19] The groups currently showing a trend of increasing in proportion to the whole are Hispanic/Latino and multiracial groups. The breakdown of children under the age of 18 by race in 2021 is shown in figure 4. Children of color comprise 51 percent of the entire child population. 26 percent of them are Hispanic or Latino. Children of Asian origin are the third largest group of color.[20]

---

17. Jones, *End of White Christian America*, 40.
18. Jones, *End of White Christian America*, 41.
19. Kids Count, "Child Population by Race, 2012–2021."
20. Portes and Rumbaut, *Immigrant America*, 264, 267.

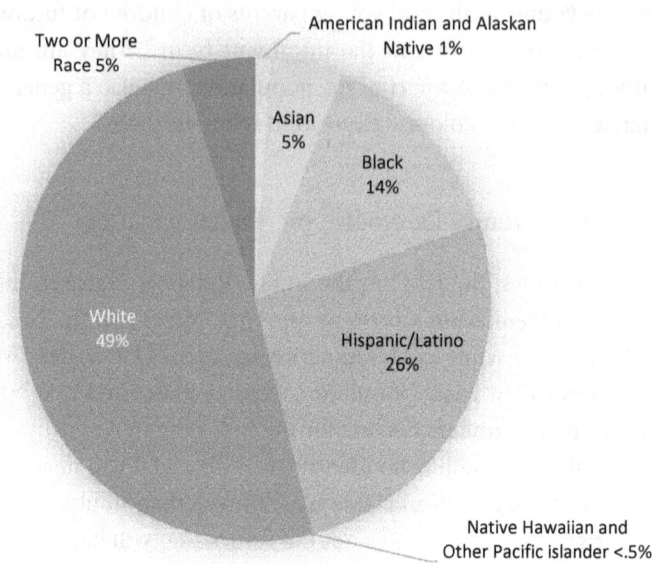

Figure 4. A breakdown of the child population in the US by race, 2021

Based on this data, when my research subjects, Gen Z and Gen Alpha Korean Americans, become adults, they will be living in a society with no racial or ethnic majority. Since these demographics are different from those of fifty or one hundred years ago, when Gen Alphas become adults and create their own families, the society will be more colorful, with multiracial families and children. This is not a forecast for the future, but a reality. Children already live in such a colorful society.

Such generational and demographic changes are not only socioculturally distinguished. In the field of ethnic studies and immigrant history, scholars are talking about new generations. Since the late 1990s, many scholars have been discussing the new second generation.[21] Chinese American sociologist Min Zhou analyzes the new second generation in several articles and books. Min Zhou and Carl L. Bankston III, in their book *The Rise of the New Second Generation*, describe two great immigrant waves in the US in the twentieth century. The turning point that distinguishes these two waves is the amendment to immigration policy in 1965 that abolished the quota system based on national origin. According to Zhou and Bankston's definition, the children of immigrants who entered the United States in the first

---

21 Jeung, Chen, and Park, "Identities of the New Second Generation," 4; Portes and Rumbaut, *Immigrant America*, 264.

wave are called the "old second generation," and the children of immigrants who entered the country after the 1965 Immigration Act are classified as "the new second generation."[22] Zhou and Bankston point out that "the old second generation was largely white and of European origin and settled in a nation that defined race mostly in terms of white and black. The new second generation is heavily non-white and non-black as these categories have been traditionally defined."[23] In her article, "Growing Up American: The Challenge Confronting Immigrant Children and Children of Immigrants," Zhou describes the new second generation as "extraordinarily diverse in national origins, socioeconomic circumstances, and settlement patterns."[24]

The data presented by the Pew Research Center (figure 5) supports the conclusions of Zhou and Bankston. Since the 1960s, European immigration has sharply decreased, while immigration from Asia and Latin America has grown rapidly.[25] Zhou and Bankston conclude, "This means that the world of the children of immigrants is not simply one of immigrant families and an existing host country, but of children of immigrants surrounded by other children of immigrants and facing a host society in rapid demographic transformation."[26] Such an analysis of the racial and cultural diversity in the world of new second generation children resonates with the studies on Generation Z. Nonetheless, Zhou and Bankston's study on the new second generation is not specifically concerned with the sociocultural characteristics of Gen Z and Gen Alpha. The new second generation, as they say, is a collective concept of all immigrants of color, and, "By now [2016], the oldest cohort of the new generation has already matured into midlife, and many have teenaged children of their own."[27] Considering this reality, understandings of the new second generation cannot be applied precisely to my research group. In other words, the lives of the Shin Yi Se embody all the trajectories named above.

---

22. Zhou and Bankston, *Rise of the New Second Generation*, 40.

23. Zhou and Bankston, *Rise of the New Second Generation*, 40; See also M. Zhou, "Growing Up American," 65.

24. M. Zhou, "Growing Up American," 65.

25. Budiman and Ruiz, "Key Facts about Asian Americans."

26. Zhou and Bankston, *Rise of the New Second Generation*, 39–40.

27. Zhou and Bankston, *Rise of the New Second Generation*, 178.

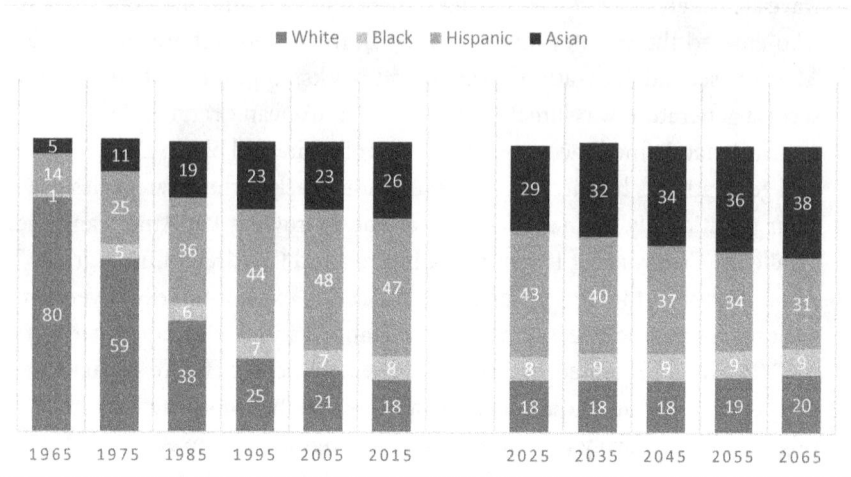

Figure 5. Percentages of immigrants by race and projections[28]

I have provided a sociocultural analysis of different generations and drawn a picture of the overall flow of immigrant demographics. Next, I will look more closely at the history of Korean immigration and the demographics and characteristics of Korean immigrants.

KOREAN IMMIGRANTS

Sociologist Jung Ha Kim, in her book *Bridge-Makers and Cross-Bearers*, describes the history of Korean immigration as having three periods. The first period was Korean immigration to Hawaii from 1903 to 1905 and to the mainland from 1910 to 1924. Around nine hundred Koreans, who were mainly intellectuals or political refugees who opposed colonial oppression, immigrated to the United States from South Korea in the early 1900s.[29]

The second wave was those Koreans who immigrated from 1951 to 1964; this period is often called "post-Korean-War immigration."[30] Immigrants of this period are divided into three groups, which include about twelve thousand "war brides" and "war orphans."[31] Most of the "war brides,"

28. Budiman and Ruiz, "Key Facts about Asian Americans."
29. J. H. Kim, *Bridge-Makers and Cross-Bearers*, 4–5.
30. J. H. Kim, *Bridge-Makers and Cross-Bearers*, 5.
31. J. H. Kim, *Bridge-Makers and Cross-Bearers*, 5.

meaning Korean wives of US servicemen who entered the United States, were not equipped with employment skills or vocational training, and they were not prepared for the language or culture of the US. In the case of "war orphans" who had been adopted by American parents, they were nurtured in American culture and parented with little opportunity to access Korean culture.[32] The third group in the post-war period was about six thousand students.[33] These students were the first group of Korean international students, who were able to study in the US with the benefit of various scholarships and special programs. Although immigrants of this period entered the United States at a similar time, they had very different immigration situations and backgrounds, so it is hard to describe them as one group.

Koreans who have immigrated since the Immigration Act of 1965 are considered the third wave.[34] They are characterized as "professional" or "family" immigrants with high education levels and strong economic backgrounds.[35] Greer Anne Wenh-In Ng notes that this third wave of Korean and Chinese immigrants "resulted in large numbers of first-generation immigrants. Many of these immigrants communicate best in their original languages while their social practices more closely reflect those of their countries of origin than those of their host countries."[36]

According to the Pew Research Center, in 2019, there were 1,908,000 Koreans or Korean Americans residing in the United States.[37] Among them, 59 percent were foreign born and 41 percent were born in the US.[38] Figure 6 shows their age distributions according to their birthplaces. As is evident in this graph, the age distribution of immigrants and US-born Korean Americans have an inverse relationship. That is, while the majority of the first generation of immigrants is older, US-born Korean Americans are primarily youth or young adults. This reveals not only the age differences but also the cultural differences between the first and second generations.

---

32. J. H. Kim, *Bridge-Makers and Cross-Bearers*, 5.
33. J. H. Kim, *Bridge-Makers and Cross-Bearers*, 6.
34. Zhou and Kim, "Community Forces and Educational Achievement," 12.
35. I. J. Kim, "Century of Korean Immigration," 30.
36. Ng, "Master Teacher to Mutual Learner," 309.
37. Budiman, "Koreans in the U.S. Fact Sheet."
38. Budiman, "Koreans in the U.S. Fact Sheet."

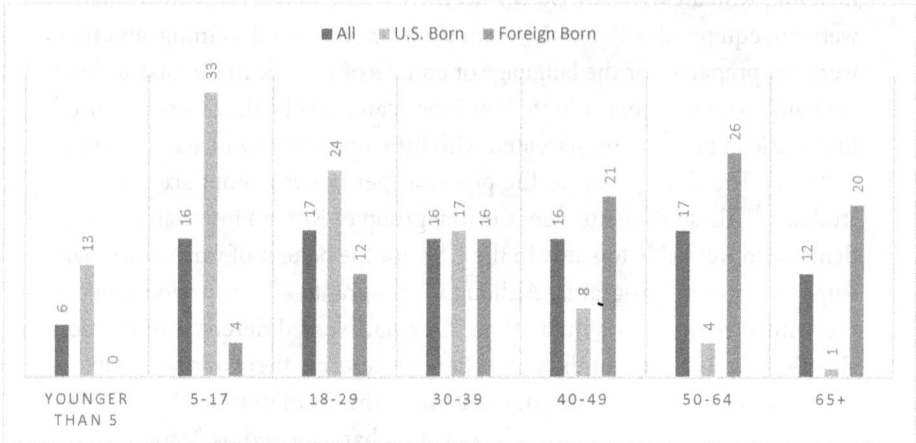

Figure 6. Ages of US Koreans in 2019, by percent of Korean population[39]

Of the total number of Korean Americans who are over twenty-five years of age, 77 percent have attained college degrees or above (see the table below).[40] For US-born Korean Americans, that figure is 87 percent.[41] Since level of education has a close relationship to later occupation and annual income, it is a significant measure of the degree of social settlement of the immigrant community.[42]

	High school or less	Some college	Bachelor's degree	Postgrad degree
All Korean Americans	23%	20%	35%	22%
US born	13%	24%	39%	24%
Foreign born	26%	19%	34%	21%
All Asians	27%	19%	30%	24%
All Americans	39%	29%	20%	13%

Overall, Korean Americans have a higher education level than the US average. The percentage of Korean Americans with some college and above

39. Budiman, "Koreans in the U.S. Fact Sheet."
40. Budiman, "Koreans in the U.S. Fact Sheet."
41. Budiman, "Koreans in the U.S. Fact Sheet."
42. Fong, *Contemporary Asian American Experience*, 62–73.

is even slightly higher than that of Asians in general. This phenomenon is closely related to the high interest in social mobility through education found in Korean culture. Zhou and Bankston discuss how second-generation children, especially Chinese and Korean children, move socially upward, beyond the social status of their parents:

> To explain why immigrant Chinese or Korean children generally do better in school than immigrant Mexican or Central American children, even when they come from families with similar income levels, live in the same neighborhood, and go to the same school, one must look at the unique contexts within which these children grow up. Among the various contextual factors that may significantly influence academic outcomes, one stands out among Chinese and Koreans—an ethnic community with an extensive system of supplementary education, including nonprofit ethnic language schools and private institutions, academic tutoring, enrichment, standardized test drills, college preparation and counseling, and extracurricular activities aimed mainly at enhancing the competitiveness of children's higher educational prospects.[43]

Of course, those who have worked hard and achieved socially deserve compliments. Yet, we should also pay attention to the issues that exist behind such educational investment. It should not be overlooked that children are pushed so hard to succeed that they are often burdened by a sense of guilt over perceived failures. The pressure for educational achievement that children feel at home is serious and often becomes overbearing in a society where racial discrimination and racial stereotypes still exist. The tensions that second-generation Korean American children feel in their homes, churches, and society can be summarized in the following two ways: education fever and racialization and marginalization.

Tension I: Education Fever

In the lives of Korean immigrant families, parents' yearnings for a better life turn into extreme expectations for their children. Such yearning is one of the reasons immigrants try to give their children more educational opportunities. In fact, historically, educational achievement was the only way to move upward socially in Korea. Korea's public education system is based on Confucian ideology, and during the Joseon Dynasty (before the advent

---

43. Zhou and Bankston, *Rise of the New Second Generation*, 76.

of modern Korea), the examination system for the selection of public officers was solely based on literacy in the humanities and Confucian ideology. It is for this reason that Koreans have believed for hundreds of years that education alone is the key to upward social mobility. The modern Korean educational system has been influenced by this heritage, and a strong bond between academic success and family honor has been formed.[44]

Most children in Korean immigrant families are considered "extensions of parental dreams."[45] Living with the pressure of parents' expectations for social mobility is normative among second-generation Korean American children and youth. Such a tendency is also depicted in the book *Minor Feelings*, written by Cathy Park Hong. As a second-generation Korean American, Hong describes the struggles that she and other Korean friends living in a Koreatown had to go through both at home and in society. She observes, "The wealthier Korean parents . . . [were] ruthlessly managing the careers and marriages of their children, and as a result ruining their children's lives, all because they wanted bragging rights."[46] Most Korean parents want their children to pursue professional degrees, especially in the areas of law, medicine, computer science, and education, so they can achieve high standards of living.[47] For Koreans in a culture of collectivism, choosing a career path is not simply an individual choice for success, but a choice for the achievement of the whole family.[48]

In "Second-Generation Korean American Christians' Communities," an essay by sociologists Sharon Kim and Rebecca Kim, an excerpt of an interview provides a view of the typical relationship between first-generation Korean immigrant parents and their children:

> As one of the SGKAs [second-generation Korean Americans] in our own study similarly explains, "Most of us have first-generation parents. We know what goes on in a Korean house: . . . parents' pressure; study, study, study; marry a Korean; don't talk back. So it is easier to get closer with other Koreans. They know where you are coming from . . . Korean parents are like, 'You have to do this, this, this to be successful . . . You have to go to medical school or law school and study, study, study.' They think the best colleges are

---

44. Rishi, "Education Fever," 2; Paik, "Introduction and International Perspectives," 542.
45. Everist, "Who Is the Child?" 65.
46. Hong, *Minor Feelings*, 118.
47. S. J. Lee, *Unraveling the "Model Minority" Stereotype*, 11.
48. Shin, *Beyond Colorblind*, 9.

Harvard, Yale, Princeton. I am not saying white people don't stress education, but Koreans, they take it to another level."[49]

Similar narratives appear in other research studies.[50] Considering that Kim and Kim's study was done within Korean American congregations, the issue of educational achievement and social success is a common conversation in the church community as well. Chih-Chieh Chou, professor of political science, argues that the success through educational achievement framework is not only based on the Confucian ethos but is reinforced by Protestant ethics:

> Immigrants from China, Japan, and Korea have brought the positive values of work, education, merit and family orientation—similar to the Protestant ethic—to an environment that substantially unburdens them of the negative Confucian values of authoritarianism, hegemony of the bureaucrats, and disdain for economic activity . . . Thus it is safe to say that the model minority myth is founded upon a supposition that Asian Americans rearticulate their 'traditional Confucian values', and their success lies in their ability to adapt their Asian values and work ethics in order to survive the American capitalist system.[51]

Eleanor Ty, an Asian Canadian and a professor of English and film studies, describes the model minority discourse as a type of self-affirmative action. Ty explains that "it assumes that [an] individual can transcend specific historical and material conditions in order to achieve happiness. The need for structural change, for governmental support of programs that enable minority groups to gain equal access to privileges usually accorded to dominant groups, is thus elided."[52] The pressure of their parents' expectations to succeed—in other words, their internalized cultural mindset as the model minority—meets additional forms of tension as second-generation children encounter racial discrimination and marginalization at school and at work.[53]

---

49. Kim and Kim, "Korean American Christians' Communities," 181.
50. S. J. Lee, *Unraveling the "Model Minority" Stereotype*, 11; Tse, "'Suffering' of the Model Minority."
51. Chou, "Notion of Model Minority," 222; S. Kim, *Faith of Our Own*, 74.
52. Ty, *Asianfail*, 3.
53. Ty, *Asianfail*, 7; S. C. Kim, "Model Minority in Distress," 63.

Tension II: Racialization and Marginalization

Many scholars of critical race theory argue that race is used as a tool of sociohistorical oppression by categorizing people according to skin color and cultural prejudice in order to strengthen and maintain the privileges of the dominant racial group.[54] Stacey J. Lee, professor of educational policy studies and Asian American studies, argues that the racial stereotype of Asian Americans as the model minority is also being used as a "hegemonic device" in sociocultural and political terms.[55] This stereotype imagines Asian American children as hard-working, high-achieving, and self-sufficient students, based on their Asian cultural background that values family and education.[56] Timothy P. Fong, professor of ethnic studies, in his book *The Contemporary Asian American Experience: Beyond the Model Minority*, points out how these stereotypes are revealed in US society and among Asian Americans, "especially in terms of exceptional educational achievements and phenomenal economic upward mobility."[57]

Asian American individuals have varying opinions about the stereotypical view of them.[58] On the positive side, this view seems to be a beneficial factor that strengthens the self-esteem of individuals and communities who are living as ethnic minorities in the US, and it keeps them from living with negative images given to them. According to a survey study on the model minority stereotype among Asian American students at one high school conducted by Stacey J. Lee, a Chinese American scholar

---

54. Choi and Lim, "Korean Newcomer Youth's Experiences," 167; Omi and Winant, *Racial Formation in the United States*, 55–56; Hartlep and Ellis, "The 'Model Minority' Myth," 340; G. J. Kim, *Embracing the Other*, 37.

55. S. J. Lee, *Unraveling the "Model Minority" Stereotype*, 6. Jean Kim points out that "a growing number of Asian American legal scholars . . . [argue] that race is not simply an immutable biological attribute (as in skin color) but represents a complex set of social meanings which are affected by political struggle (Omi and Winant 1994). Understanding that race is socially and politically, rather than biologically, determined may help us to understand how racial prejudice and racial dominance operate in U.S. society." J. Kim, "Asian American Identity Development Theory," 68.

56. Lee and Zhou, *Asian American Achievement Paradox*, 9, 116; Sue and Kitano, "Stereotypes as a Measure of Success," 95; G. S. Kim, "Asian North American Immigrant Parents and Youth," 135; G. J. Kim, *Embracing the Other*, 50.

57. Fong, *Contemporary Asian American Experience*, 62.

58. S. J. Lee, *Unraveling the "Model Minority" Stereotype*, 12; S. C. Kim, "Model Minority in Distress," 62.

in education policies, Korean students and their parents accept the model minority stereotype as a positive image and one to be proud of.[59]

However, despite this positive side, the attitude behind this image that still classifies Asians as "minority" foreigners should not be overlooked. The term *model minority* signals that in achieving these educational and economic successes, Asian Americans are a minority race that can be a "model," not a "problem," for other ethnic minorities, because they have done well on their own, without government initiatives or support.[60] In her article, "Continuing Significance of the Model Minority Myth: The Second Generation," sociologist Lisa Sun-Hee Park states,

> The model minority myth is a seemingly positive image that seduces both liberal and conservative political inclinations. The moral "pull yourself up by your bootstraps" lessons regarding individual responsibility and upward economic mobility derived from this imagery continue to hold favor in the current movement to dismantle the social welfare state. The model minority myth wholly endorses the American Dream of meritocracy and democracy with the notion that anyone regardless of race, class, or gender has an equal opportunity to work hard and consequently is justly rewarded for their labor though economic upward mobility. Intrinsic to this myth is the fact that a model minority is a minority nonetheless; racial minorities can pull their bootstraps only so far—tokens notwithstanding.[61]

The model minority stereotype, combined with complex problems among Asian Americans and between them and other racial minorities, has caused many Asian Americans to keep silent about their diverse experiences and needs.[62] In addition, it is problematic that there are many immi-

---

59. Lee notes, "Korean students told me that they and their parents were proud of being represented as model minorities. They resented all Asians who risked destroying the model minority image for them. They had, in other words, consented to the hegemonic discourse of the model minority stereotype." S. J. Lee, *Unraveling the "Model Minority" Stereotype*, 30.

60. Fong, *Contemporary Asian American Experience*, 62; Hartlep and Ellis, "The 'Model Minority' Myth," 344; Hong, *Minor Feelings*, 22; Lee and Zhou, *Asian American Achievement Paradox*, 176–78.

61. Lisa Park, "Significance of the Model Minority Myth," 498. See also Kawai, "Stereotyping Asian Americans," 114.

62. S. J. Lee, *Unraveling the "Model Minority" Stereotype*, 8, 12; S. C. Kim, "Model Minority in Distress," 63–64; Chou, "Notion of Model Minority," 219–20; Shin, *Beyond Colorblind*, 46; Sue and Kitano, "Stereotypes as a Measure of Success," 83–98; Fong,

grant parents who misunderstand and internalize such a racist stereotype as a positive status that they and their children must achieve. As Stacey Lee argues, "Self-silencing and the uncritical acceptance of the model minority stereotype represent Asian American consent to hegemony."[63] Without facing and improving social structural issues and trying to break through invisible racial boundaries, emphasizing an individual's ability and effort simply deepens the problem and "can create undue pressure and unhealthy levels of psychological and emotional stress on young students."[64] This issue was also revealed in my ethnographic research on Korean Americans. I will further discuss parents' internalized racism and educational expectations of their children in chapter four.

In a similar vein, the images of the "yellow peril" and the "perpetual foreigner" keep Asian Americans marginalized from mainstream society, even if they were born and raised in the US for generations, by subtly subordinating them within racial boundaries and keeping them out of major discussions on race and social justice.[65] Grace Ji-Sun Kim, a Korean American theologian, in her book *Embracing the Other*, asserts that the "yellow peril exemplifies overt racism while the model minority myth functions as covert racism."[66] As strongly interlocked forms of racism, the model minority stereotype and the yellow peril image inseparably work together against Asian Americans, not only in the white mainstream society but also within other groups of color.[67] The implicitly institutionalized racial stereotype of the yellow peril that sees Asians as outsiders greatly influences

---

Contemporary Asian American Experience, 62–63; Kawai, "Stereotyping Asian Americans," 113–14.

63. S. J. Lee, *Unraveling the "Model Minority" Stereotype*, 12. She adds, "In addition to silencing the diverse experiences and concerns of Asian Americans, the model minority stereotype implicitly denies Asian American experiences with racism. Here, the success of some Asian Americans is used to support the idea that Asian Americans do not face racial barriers" (12). See also Hartlep and Ellis, "The 'Model Minority' Myth," 335–36.

64. Fong, *Contemporary Asian American Experience*, 93; Lee and Zhou, *Asian American Achievement Paradox*, 70–71; Hartlep and Ellis, "The 'Model Minority' Myth," 337; Choi and Lim, "Korean Newcomer Youth's Experiences," 173–74.

65. S. J. Lee, *Unraveling the "Model Minority" Stereotype*, 5–6; Zhou and Bankston, *Rise of the New Second Generation*, 40; Jeung, Chen, and Park, "Identities of the New Second Generation," 7; S. C. Kim, "Model Minority in Distress," 63; J. Kim, "Asian American Identity Development Theory," 70–71; Shin, *Beyond Colorblind*, 113; G. J. Kim, *Invisible*, 62.

66. G. J. Kim, *Embracing the Other*, 51.

67. G. J. Kim, *Embracing the Other*, 165.

the emotional stability and identity formation of Asian Americans.[68] Both stereotypes create the psychological desire to be assimilated into the white mainstream society, while silently covering up the reality of racial discrimination against Asian Americans. Here, one of the serious psychological problems that arises is racial identity conflict.[69] The racial identity conflict is not only a matter of individual identity formation, but also of racial/ethnic conflicts with other racial/ethnic groups.

Koreans' exclusiveness and sense of superiority over other Asian people should be discussed within the framework of the geopolitical location of Korea, its long history, and cultural studies. Stacey Lee found in her research on the educational experiences of Asian American youth that Korean-identified students considered themselves "better than other Asian Americans because they were from higher social-class backgrounds than most of the Southeast Asians."[70] She observed that students learned such "attitudes about Korean superiority and social class from their parents."[71] An extensive discussion of this issue is beyond the scope of this study, which is more focused on the combination of and conflict between the internalized model minority mindset and Confucian elitism. Therefore, I will leave it as a future research project.

Going back to my conversation with Soo Jeong at the mall, I know how pleasant it is to have my ethnic background recognized and to talk about the popular K-pop culture with someone. While I have not known much about BTS or other K-pop groups, there have been some people like Soo Jeong who have come up to me and talked to me about Korean songs or Korean dramas on Netflix. Yet, I dream of a day when people recognize and talk about many different Asian celebrities and ethnic cultures. I dream of a day when the second and following generations of Asian American children and youth freely claim their voice and purpose, find their ontological vocations, and joyfully and confidently take their own journeys in the world. There is still a long way to go in this time of fear and hatred in the world. Yet, the day is coming. The day is coming.

---

68. G. J. Kim, *Embracing the Other*, 107; G. J. Kim, *Invisible*, 62.
69. J. Kim, "Asian American Identity Development Theory," 69.
70. S. J. Lee, *Unraveling the "Model Minority" Stereotype*, 28.
71. S. J. Lee, *Unraveling the "Model Minority" Stereotype*, 29.

Chapter 2

"SO KOREAN" WHEREVER YOU ARE

ON A SUNDAY MORNING

After the children's worship service at a suburban Korean United Methodist Church, the children went to their classes along with their teachers. When I entered the class of second- and third-graders, the nine children put their own bags and jackets on hooks on the wall and sat around the table. They were sitting on adult-sized chairs and could not reach the floor with their feet. They playfully swung their legs under the table. A youth student who was serving as a teacher's assistant (TA) took attendance and helped a child who had not been able to find a seat yet, putting the child's bag and jacket on a hook.

The teacher brought out the charts the class used the week before, and briefly reminded the students about the season of Lent. Then the teacher introduced the day's theme, kindness, and asked the children to think about how they could be kind to others, just as Jesus was kind to them. The teacher distributed a handout, which was from a ready-made curriculum kit. The handout was about how the children could choose to be kind to others during the coming week. A girl in the corner only glanced at the handout she had been given and then began drawing something on it. The children could not easily answer the teacher's questions about how they could be kind and seemed unable to concentrate. A couple minutes later, the teacher began giving some examples of responses: "What about washing dishes after dinner? That's one idea."

Sean, who was chatting with a friend and looking for something to play with, had already been called out several times by the teacher for his behavior. He was told to sit quietly and concentrate on the lesson. The TA quietly approached Sean from behind so he could watch over him. The teacher said, "Your brother wants to play with your game player. Then, what do you say to him? Or . . ." As the examples continued, Sean, cupping his chin in his hands, said, "My brother's mean to me all the time. I don't want to forgive him. How can I be kind to him?" His face reddened. He muttered and continued to talk about what his brother did to him, but the class couldn't hear his voice clearly. The teacher responded to him using the lesson's theme: "Because Jesus was kind to us. Should we not be kind to other people, regardless? We're practicing Jesus's way." The teacher continued, speaking to the class, "How about this; can you think about times when people were kind to you? That you were thankful. You know what, sometimes people are mean to us, sometimes they are not. Most of the time, they are not."

The teacher put some answers, such as cleaning, smiling, and washing dishes, on the whiteboard and moved on to the next activity, which was to fill out the handout. The teacher said, "How can you be nice and kind to other people, at school, at home, or at a market? Think about it and write down your own answers on the sheet, then pick one that you will do next week."

Alex cautiously raised his hand, saying, "Can I say something else?"

"You want to say something? Okay. Go ahead."

"We are not friends with any of them [Muslim classmates] and I am not gonna be. There's somebody in my class and they are learning some things in their church—I mean, their church is for Islam—and he says Christmas is not right, and every single one of us who go to church is wrong."

"What did YOU say?" the teacher asked.

While other children were working on their handouts, the conversation between the teacher and Alex continued. Alex said, "I said, 'That's okay. That's your opinion.'"

The teacher responded, "You know what, I think that's also an act of kindness, instead of responding 'You're wrong.' You said everyone has their own opinion, right?"

"But he keeps saying annoying things."

"That's okay. But are you responding meanly to him or saying, 'Be quiet; leave me alone'? Or, do you tell him, 'I understand you as a friend,' right? Even though he annoyed you, you responded with kindness. Did you respond that you were annoyed or did you respond, 'I understand that's what you are saying?' Keep responding politely. That's one way to act kindly toward other people."

Alex returned to his work, and the teacher continued to the next part of the lesson. The teacher checked the students' homework and whether they knew the previous week's memory verse, then let the children recite that day's memory verse twice. By the end of the forty-five-minute lesson, the environment was excessively noisy, the teacher's voice was getting hoarse, and his face was getting red. When the session was over, the teacher looked obviously tired but sent the children out to their parents with a smile.

On that Sunday morning, with the rain falling outside, the lower level of the church where the children were briskly coming and going was exceptionally noisy. The Bible study rooms built around the children's worship room were each suitable for about eight adults, with a whiteboard and adult-sized folding chairs and tables. But the walls between the rooms were so thin that the noises of the other rooms were excessively loud and distracting in any particular room. In such a room, there is typically insufficient space to maneuver when it is filled with eight to ten children sitting around a table, along with an adult teacher and a youth TA.

This illustration of a children's Sunday school class reveals several issues that are common in Korean American churches. For a teacher who was prepared only to deposit biblical knowledge and maybe answer some simple questions, a child's anxiety about how to interact with a Muslim friend was more than the teacher could cope with. Yet, it shows one of the most common issues that second-generation Asian American Christian children experience at school. Teachers, as well as parents, are not prepared to deal with the questions and challenges children bring to the table. In this chapter, this illustration will be reflected on from various angles, as it reveals some key issues with Korean Christian education, such as the banking model of education described by Paulo Freire, and how Confucian morality, internalized racism, and racial stereotypes are embedded in the Korean immigrant church and its education programs.

PORTRAITS OF THE SITES

Korean American churches are located at the intersections of religion and cultures, languages, generations, and Korean immigrant history in the United States. The Korean American church is not only a place of worship and faith formation, but it is also an incubator of sociocultural relationships for Korean immigrants and later generations. Korean American churches are base camps of redemptive community at the center of immigrants' lives in the midst of a globalizing society. In this chapter, based on interviews and participatory observations conducted in two Korean congregations in the southeast region of the US, I present how Korean American churches live, struggle, and incubate new possibilities in the lives of first- and 1.5-generation Korean immigrants and their young children.

In their article titled "Second-Generation Korean American Christians' Communities," sociologists Sharon Kim and Rebecca Y. Kim propose four main models of ethnic churches: (1) the classic model of an ethnic cultural hub, (2) the assimilated or accommodated church model, (3) *de facto* congregations, and (4) pan-ethnic congregations.[1] The first model of the church is geared toward first-generation immigrants. Second-generation children joining the Korean-speaking service continue to be influenced by the ethnic culture. In the second model, the first-generation parents and the second-generation children coexist in one church building, but there are some ministries in English. Congregations following the third model have a separate ministry leadership and service for the second generation, yet share the building space with the first generation. The fourth model describes pan-Asian congregations that have gone beyond the existing models of immigrant churches. According to Kim and Kim, "continuing racial divisions in the broader society lead to the construction of separate Asian churches that join together ethnic groups such as Chinese Americans, Korean Americans, and Japanese Americans."[2] They also note that there are sub-models they have found in their studies and that the four main models of ethnic churches can overlap as churches transition from one to another.[3]

Among these four representative models, Future Korean UMC[4] fits the third model of a *de facto* congregation. Starting with the first model, it

---

1. Kim and Kim, "Korean American Christians' Communities," 177–79.
2. Kim and Kim, "Korean American Christians' Communities," 179.
3. Kim and Kim, "Korean American Christians' Communities," 177, 178.
4. "Future Korean UMC" and "Hope Korean UMC" are pseudonyms for the churches

transitioned to the second, then to the third as the members' children grew up and moved on. But there is no English worship service for adults and young adults now, since the second-generation congregation has moved out to another location. Hope Korean UMC is an illustration of the second model, an assimilated or accommodated church. As the number of English-speaking youths grew, there was a natural increase in the number of young adults and the need to expand the church's ministry for them. With some newcomers who are young English-speaking couples and families, its English ministry is growing. The minister of the English ministry is also a second-generation Korean American, someone who has graduated from a seminary and been ordained in the UMC.

In both churches, the adults' services are held in Korean (the Korean service), and the children's and youth's services are offered in English. So, when a service is called "the English ministry" or "the English service," this refers to the age or generation of the primary worship participants. There are some Korean churches in the southeastern US that offer all their services in Korean, respecting their mother language and claiming a stronger identity as "Korean" churches. In that regard, having English services for children, youth, and young adults reveals a tendency toward the second model of an ethnic church, the accommodated or assimilated model.

The major findings of my study of Korean American churches and the religious education they provide clustered around four themes: (1) family and community-oriented lifestyle, (2) aging congregations and a generation gap, (3) banking-model education and a lack of effort to provide faith formation for all ages, and (4) internalization of the racial stereotype of the model minority.

"SO KOREAN": FAMILY AND COMMUNITY-ORIENTED LIFESTYLE

I asked all my interviewees why they joined Future Korean UMC or Hope Korean UMC instead of one of the other Korean congregations in the area. Although most of them already had a Christian (Catholic or Protestant) influence in their past, some said they had only begun attending church after coming to the United States. Their denominational backgrounds were also very diverse. I asked first-generation members why they had come to their particular church, particularly since they had immigrated. And I asked

---

I observed.

why the 1.5-generation members had settled in a first-generation-centered church. The most common answer to these questions was "just because." It was just because they were looking for a Korean ethnic church in the area they were settling into and just because the worship style and the sermons of the lead pastor touched their hearts. Emily shared,

> I was not a devout Christian [before I came to the US]. But people told me that I would need a Korean community while living in the US. So, people were saying I'd better to go to a Korean church. In Korea, I sometimes went to a Catholic church, and one of my close friends invited me to a Protestant church. Then I came to the US [before going to the Protestant church with her friend]. But I was still told that it was good to go to a Korean church here in the US, and my husband was also thinking of attending a church. "So, yes, let's go for sure," we said. So, we arrived in the US and we were staying in a hotel for a few weeks. So, we, our entire family, with an eighteen-month-old baby, went to church on that Sunday. Then there was Pastor Park and I liked the atmosphere of the church. It was very good. As soon as I first came to church, I liked the calm atmosphere. Since I was used to the Catholic style, I liked the more calm and traditional style, rather than being in the too loud or contemporary worship service.

For Emily and Kyung, it was a very natural, straightforward process to find a Korean American church community where they could blend in, with no barriers of language and culture, while they had to deal with a different language and culture in their daily lives.

Alice and Jay, 1.5-generation immigrants, replied that "there was no reason," when I asked why they had not chosen another ethnic or multiethnic congregation. I was particularly interested in these respondents, who were 1.5 generation and perfectly bilingual. It was my assumption that the 1.5 generation would have more diverse choices, as they were relatively in between cultural boundaries and had various possibilities and access, unlike first-generation immigrants who would have relatively fewer choices to find a community where they could share the same emotions and language with others as they settled down in the US. Yet, Alice and Jay still decided to remain in Korean immigrant congregations where Korean religious and cultural values were more abundant. I realized that ethnic and cultural familiarity is one of the top priorities individuals have when they are selecting a religious community. Alice even said she had never thought about visiting other ethnic churches, as is evident in her response to my follow-up question:

> Me: If . . . your child wants to see children of diverse cultures in their faith, can you go to an American church together? You can serve there; there are enough similarities [in terms of language and culture]; you would not have any difficulties.
> Alice: But the service and the faith are different. If I want, I can do volunteer work at my work or at my kid's school. I don't particularly feel any need to join an American church in order to provide that spiritual experience to my children.[5]

During my interviews with the 1.5-generation participants, I noticed that they chose a community of faith based on their emotional comfort and sense of security, rather than choosing a church based on any serious reflection on theology or community composition. They were rather puzzled about my question about going to an American church and asked what I meant or intended. Here, it is notable that Kim and Kim explain the tendency of second-generation Korean Americans to choose and stay in Korean communities:

> As a pastor in our own study explains, "In the Christian community we call it the homogeneous principle: . . . people want to worship with people who are like them." This is part of the broader sociological principle of what sociologists refer to as homophily—the idea that "similarity breeds connection," that ties between similar individuals are more binding, or more proverbially, that "birds of a feather flock together" (McPherson, Smith-Lovin, and Cook 2001, 415; Duncan, Featherman, and Duncan 1972; Marsden 1987; Park and Burgess 1921). Following these patterns of group association, 1.5- and second-generation Korean American pastors are creating their own faith communities, spaces of worship that uniquely resonate with today's SGKAs [second-generation Korean Americans].[6]

According to Kim and Kim's study, it is a common tendency for people to seek out a homogeneous group where they can blend in for their religious life. In my interviews, there was no one who could articulate why it is important or why it is not important to stay in a Korean congregation.

---

5. When we said "American church" in our conversations, we implicitly agreed that it meant a majority white congregation.

6. Kim and Kim, "Korean American Christians' Communities," 184.

Yet, they preferred community experiences among people who shared the same culture, history, and language, and they did not feel a need to have cross-cultural, cross-racial worship experiences.

The cultural tendency to assimilate and to try to belong within mainstream culture as a minority race was not revealed in my interviews. Religious life remains in the private sector, and it is the role of the ethnic church to create a space for congregants to experience comfort and support in their native culture, away from the pressures to be assimilated and affiliated with the host society. My interviewees felt satisfied with their choice to stay in Korean churches to meet their spiritual needs and to have an ethnic network, while at the same time assimilating into the host society for social interaction. Sociologist Jung Ha Kim explains such a tendency as "adhesive adaptation," meaning the two different cultures coexist in the life of immigrants.[7] The emphasis on cultural solidarity also reveals the family- and community-centered lifestyle of Korean culture, with its basis in Confucianism. Eunju shared, "I wish that our daughter, Jihyun, would grow up and respect her parents and cherish the church life as much as we do." In this statement, Eunju revealed how family and the church community have the same important value for them. This understanding was often revealed in other interviews as well. Parents emphasized the importance of family and community as well as wishing for the happiness of their children. Kay expressed these values in his son's words—"so Korean"—meaning the tendency of Korean people to always gather, argue, and struggle with each other, but still not leaving for cross-cultural, cross-racial communities. It is a short and somewhat cynical and humorous description of the tendency of Koreans to prioritize ethnic solidarity while adjusting to the culture of the host society.

However, adults are not the only ones who feel safe in an ethnic church; several interviewees noted that their children also felt emotionally comfortable in the Korean American community:

> Min: But that's different for each kid. In the case of my son, he is not interested in being with a Korean or not. Maybe he would be more comfortable with Koreans . . . Maybe he will be a little, as he is not so interested in interaction with others. But my daughter is much more comfortable being with other Korean kids.
>
> Emily: When you come to the church, you do not usually see it, but since there are all Korean people, it just comforts your heart.

---

7. J. H. Kim, *Bridge-Makers and Cross-Bearers*, 14.

> Kids feel the same. No matter how long they have been in the United States, no matter how much the American culture or the way of thinking is comfortable at school, once they come to the Korean church where there are Koreans, I have heard that they feel somehow comfortable and stable. There are some children who explicitly feel it, or implicitly for some others kids. That is why I think it is important for the pastors and teachers to embrace them with love and faith [so the kids feel emotional support].

The ethnic-cultural experience, emotional stability, and sense of belonging in Korean churches of second-generation Koreans and their children described by Kim and Kim are confirmed in the interviews above. Kim and Kim noticed that when second-generation Korean Americans were married and had children, they wanted to have some experience with Korean culture and wanted to belong to a Korean ethnic community in addition to the American culture that they experienced in school or in the broader society. "Because racism and ethnic divisions persist, SGKAs believe that later-generation Koreans who have no understanding or connection with their Korean culture will be rootless and homeless. They too will be in their own cultural limbo."[8] Such concerns about racism and the desires of second-generation parents were also revealed in Sohee's interview:

> If you think about it, there are racially segregated communities as well as churches. I do not think that, however, will ever be solved. And I don't think we need to change it. White and black people who grow up in the US and use the same language in the same culture cannot be reconciled. Then why do Koreans [need to try to reconcile with other ethnic groups by coexisting in faith communities]? We don't have to. We just need to do our way well and to get along . . . I didn't need a community of people who speak in Korean, but I wanted to have my kids experience church with other Korean kids. So, let them feel there is a space for Korean kids. Speaking in Korean does not matter to me or my kids, but I hoped my kids would know that there are Korean communities and solidarity.

The sarcastic words of Kay's son have value in that they express the power of solidarity against racial discrimination that Korean immigrants experience. At the same time, ethnic solidarity is also a survival strategy for living in and fighting against the racism that still exists in the United States.

---

8. Kim and Kim, "Korean American Christians' Communities," 185–86.

"So Korean" Wherever You Are

AGING CONGREGATIONS AND THE GENERATION GAP

One challenge young Korean immigrant families are dealing with in the church is the disconnection between generations. In general, as in most mainline churches in the United States, the aging of Korean churches is getting more serious. Also, Future Church and Hope Church recently had a larger influx of people over the age of fifty-five than an influx of young families. The fact that the interviewees from the two churches pointed to this as a problem they had in common proves that this is a phenomenon that is noticeable enough for the entirety of each congregation to experience. Kay, a member of Future Church, talked about this situation:

> There is also an issue of the aging of this congregation. The elders in my church believe that our church is growing and reviving. At the 8:00 a.m. service [a service for older adults in general], the chapel seating is getting tighter. And the number of people in the weekday seniors' program was smaller than the Sunday school at first, but it is much bigger now. Their children, or grandchildren, are probably youth now, meaning that they don't care about the children's ministry and their issues any more. How do they know the needs of the Sunday school? Whatever the next generation does . . . They don't even know how long they can live and stay in this church. They don't care.

This aging phenomenon does not simply mean a change in the face of the congregation. It means a change in the focus of the main ministries of the church, which leads young families who are seeking ministries for younger generations to drop away. Kyung, who attended Future Church at first and moved to Hope Church for its ministry focused on the younger generation, expressed the sense of crisis due to the growing number of elderly people: "I am still the youngest in the men's group and have been for the last ten years. Of course, there are a couple of younger families, but some are just coming to the service and going, or have little babies. So . . . they are not deeply involved in ministries; we are still doing the work of the young people until the age of 40-something."

In Korean immigrant churches, which are based on a Confucian mindset and style of relationship formation, age represents another status. In such a culture, having newcomers who are relatively older does not usually mean that leaders will have a colleague who can work with younger existing members. Rather, it means they will have more people to serve. Having said that, having more older members creates a distinct dynamic in the community, because children's and youth's ministries need many volunteers who are young and active and are able to communicate with young people, preferably bilingually. Kyung's sense of crisis as the youngest member of the adult ministry, even at the age of almost fifty, reflects all these realities. His comment also raises the question of whether those of the younger generation—namely generation X—are receiving proper spiritual care and ministerial services for themselves in their congregations, beyond serving others. Kyung's next comment revealed that he has been struggling with this problem in recent years and trying to make meaning out of it:

> At first, I was quite upset and wanted to change it somehow, but now I'm thinking it could be God's will. Our church may be a church for seniors. For God's sake. . . . Nowadays, just to have comfort in mind, I try to think that God has set up our church for seniors. Because all other Korean churches in this area focus on the next generation, young generations. The seniors have no place to go. When the focus is on the English congregation, the young children, the seniors can be left out and lonely. When pastor Jang came to Hope Church and changed the format of worship from a contemporary to a traditional worship format, removed the praise band, made the choir, and let people sing hymns, not contemporary praise songs . . . then the number of congregants doubled. Most of the newcomers are in their 50s or older.

The Korean American community has a distinctive gap between generations, and within the church, there is a clear difference in the worship style or ministry preference of different age groups. This is not just a challenge found in Future Church and Hope Church, but it is also a struggle that most Korean churches go through in the transition of worship services and ministries to fit the needs of different immigrant generations. The immigrant church experience of Sarah Shin, a second-generation Korean American and a campus minister, was no different. Shin wrote, "Many churches, immigrant and not, hold on to traditions that are culturally normal for them. The conservative values of the previous generation don't necessarily appeal to the younger generations, and churches fail to change alongside our ever-evolving world."[9] Although a Korean congregation may have to worship bilingually due to language differences and change the previous, familiar worship style to a style that is unfamiliar to old-timers,

---

9. Shin, *Beyond Colorblind*, 188.

without such an effort, the church will lose those of the younger generations, as Shin warns.

The way in which generations are completely separated and worship in different languages and worship styles in many Korean congregations suggests the probability that the groups will separate into two congregations in the near future—the parents' church and the children's church. This assumption is based on the evidence that the children who grow up as Christians tend to stay in their own ethnic community. Unless church ministries redirect their paths from operations focused on the first generation, which fears changes in worship format, to a more second-generation- and children-friendly environment, and unless the perception of Korean-speaking pastors changes and Korean immigrant congregations support and invest in bilingual education pastors, the future of the Korean church in the US is uncertain.

All these findings point to the next step. Korean immigrant churches need a new approach to replace bankrupt methodologies in order to ensure the healthy faith development and identity formation of emerging new second-generation Korean American children and their families.

BANKING MODEL EDUCATION AND LACK OF FAITH FORMATION FOR ALL AGES

In his writings, Brazilian educator and philosopher Paulo Freire discusses two types of educational approaches: the traditional model of education, which he calls banking education, and his liberative model, which he calls problem-posing education. According to him, the banking model form of education reflects the atmosphere of an oppressive society. This education model, as the word *banking* suggests, is characterized by memorization and repetition and by unilateral instruction focused on the authority and power of the teacher, which is based on the assumption that the teacher possesses all the knowledge and students are ignorant.[10] In this model of education, the subject is the teacher and the students are the passive recipients.[11] On the other hand, students are the subjects in problem-posing education. In this model of education, students are engaged in dialogue so they can become critically aware of their situations and be able to articulate their

---

10. Ng, "Master Teacher to Mutual Learner," 310–31.
11. Freire, *Pedagogy of the Oppressed*, 83–84; Spring, *Wheels in the Head*, 155.

thinking in their own words.¹² The teacher tries to only talk about the students' main interests and issues and does not try to dictate or define their way of thinking.¹³ Education philosopher Joel Spring notes, "Living in a culture of silence, people do not make their lives an object of reflection. They just act without reflecting on the reasons for their actions. In Freire's terminology, they are dehumanized.... Many people living in a culture of silence, according to Freire, have never considered their lives as objects to be discussed."¹⁴ It is truly heartbreaking that this repressive, dehumanizing education is happening in Sunday school classrooms where practices of love and peace for individual and social salvation should be experienced.

Why is the problem of this one-sided educational system not solved but continued over generations? I argue that it is because there are no strong and healthy faith formation approaches designed for all age groups. Neither children nor adults have experienced another type of education, and it is evident that the banking model of worship and preaching is not encouraging faith development in any generation. John H. Westerhoff III, an Episcopal priest and the former professor of theology and Christian nurture at Duke University, has insisted that "the schooling-instructional paradigm is bankrupt."¹⁵ He declared the bankruptcy of religious education and called for an alternative religious education model more than four decades ago. And his argument is still valid.

What was revealed through my ethnographic research was the discrepancy between knowing and doing. Parents and teachers already knew that banking education was an ineffective form of faith education for themselves and their children. Adults wanted to know how to live faithful lives. Nevertheless, in educational ministries, the banking model of education is the one that is prevalent. The words Alice used in our interview were interesting to me. She said that all Christian parents want the same thing for their children—to grow into people who know God's love. I became aware of the significance of her use of the phrase *know God's love*. This expression is not unique to Alice—a perfectly bilingual 1.5-generation adult—but is a commonly used phrase in the Korean church. Among other expressions about God's love, Alice's choice of the word *know* indicates the consciousness that people, including Alice, consider it important

12. Freire, *Pedagogy of the Oppressed*, 83, 124.
13. Spring, *Wheels in the Head*, 160.
14. Spring, *Wheels in the Head*, 161.
15. Westerhoff, *Will Children Have Faith?*, 40–41.

to "know" dynamic relationships and feelings of love. Below is the conversation I had with Alice:

> Alice: It's the same. It seems to be the same whether it is a teacher or a mother. I wish my children or other children would know God's love and put it in their hearts.
>
> Me: Knowing God's love . . . Yes, it is also a task. . . . How can you apply this model [Yolanda Smith's model] to the Korean American church?
>
> Alice: Well, I do not think we've ever reached that point yet.
>
> Me: Oh, right. That's not a problem.
>
> Alice: My church may not have such a clear vision yet. Because, of course, it would be fine to have one, but I don't know when it can be achieved. But for now [in children's ministry], the kids just need to know something. They don't know anything. So we really have to start with the basic things. I think the foundation is important. So, I decided to teach about the Bible. They don't even know what's in the Old Testament and the New Testament. . . . They don't even know that.

I was quite puzzled that Alice started her class by having the children memorize the sixty-six books of the Bible. Was this part of her plan to raise children to know God's love? Will memorizing books of the Bible and Bible verses eventually lead to the growth of children as people who love God and others? God's love is not about simply knowing, but also feeling, experiencing, and practicing. And a children's education ministry should be a place where children can experience and deepen their love of God and others.

Again, the banking schooling model is bankrupt. Even though Alice is faithfully serving her church and teaching children with joy, this discrepancy between knowing and doing also reveals the limits of adult faith education. The paradigm shift to the notion of "a person who knows God's love" should begin with adult faith education, so parents and teachers can better nurture children in faith.

MODEL MINORITY COMPLEX

One of the questions I asked in my interviews was about racism. I asked all my interviewees if they had experienced any form of racial discrimination since they had come to the United States. This is because racial discrimination can be an important factor in social experiences and personality development. Interestingly, however, all of them said they hadn't experienced any kind of racism. As soon as I finished asking my question, they shook their heads and replied as if they didn't even know what racism was. At first, it was awkward and difficult to continue the conversation related to racism. Yet, while talking about other issues, Alice did bring up the topic of racism:

> There are still a few times. I can't say I didn't experience racism at all. There can be racism among many people out there. Because it is common to everybody. Nothing special. Think about how people talk. People in Nashville are generous and slow . . . then, when you go to Boston or New York, they talk so fast, act fast, and mean. So, if you go somewhere like that, even white people get discriminated against. If you think that way, nothing is hard to understand. No problem. Because I am Asian? Well . . . [shaking her head "no"].

If one has not experienced racism in life or has not been traumatized with deep wounds, this is a blessing for the individual. But what I felt through all my interviews was that the interviewees did not answer "no" because they had not experienced any kind of racial discrimination. Rather, they had experienced some degree of discrimination and segregation as a normal part of daily life and didn't want to point it out. Experiences of oppressive alienation can be hard to digest, so people sometimes close their eyes and pretend like nothing serious has happened. My participants were responding to my question about racism by assertively stating that racism is no longer an issue in the United States and that they believed the situation will be even better for their children's generation. At some points, I strongly wished this were all true.

However, this kind of paradoxical attitude—being aware of the existence and experience of racism, but regarding racism as not being very personally relevant—is not a constructive solution to the problem of the profoundly systemic racism and social injustice that exist. It does not help at all. Such a mindset of Asians, considering themselves as a relatively bright-colored race and as second-level white people, does not prevent or hide the problem of the structural racism that exists.

Continuing the conversation about racism, Alice kept speaking as if to comfort me, to persuade me, or to make excuses:

> By the way, what I see is the ability to succeed beyond race or something like that. It was the same when I was working for a company. It does not matter which school you graduated from. Back then, when I was in my 20s, I was obsessed with it [capability, social achievement]. So, when I got a job as soon as I graduated and became a proficient manager, I was so proud of myself. Think about it. Most people in the company were white and older than me; I was a young, twenty-some-year-old Asian woman . . . I thought it was my ability at the time. Looking back, that was all God's grace.

In this conversation, Alice demonstrates awareness of the difference between mainstream and non-mainstream culture, between other people's races and her own race. And she knew it could be extraordinary and rare to succeed in the mainstream society as an Asian woman, as implied by her attributing her success to "God's grace." Nonetheless, she expressed that such success in mainstream American society can be achieved through the efforts and abilities of individuals, regardless of their race or gender. Here I argue that there is a subtle combination of internalized racism and the model minority mindset in Alice's belief that one can overcome fear or the disadvantages of racism and other issues through individual effort.

What makes the area in which my participants lived more appealing to Koreans is that Korean and Asian merchants have formed a convenient living zone. Koreans living in this area feel safer and more comfortable in their Korean bubble than Koreans in other regions. In this bubble, their living needs can be satisfied, including school and religious activities. Kyung pointed this out when he said it wasn't necessary for Korean children to be friends with children of other races:

> Nowadays, kids do not think race or anything is important. For example, there are so many American children,[16] and a few Korean children in the school; they [the Korean kids] might be bullied, and this becomes an issue, but the kids are getting along with other kids of the same color and the same language. They and their parents have good communication with each other. Then this [racial discrimination or segregation] is not an issue at all. Kids consider it normal that Koreans get along with Koreans and Americans get along with Americans. Even look at Jay. Jay has been living in America for a very long time, but he likes to be with Korean people. Look at Nick. Even though he speaks in English and thinks

16. Here again, *American* means English-speaking white people.

like an American, he is more comfortable with Koreans. Then why not our kids? Why bother?

Living and interacting in an insular community provides a sense of safety and comfort. Such emotional comfort is also found in Korean churches, as discussed previously. Kyung explored this topic further:

> Future Church used to try a lot [to create cross-cultural or cross-racial relationships] . . . In American society, there are many [Korean] parents who have no reluctance about being in American culture, so [they say], "Let's invite other [Americans] to Future Church. We have nothing to hide or be ashamed of; we are as good as any high-class white people in this neighborhood. Let's invite the kids and their friends [for more socializing]." But nothing worked. In one such attempt, Peace Church [the English-speaking Korean congregation] tried to invite white friends of second-generation Korean Americans to their worship service, since it is hard to have a multiracial gathering anywhere else. They tried, hoping then they would get closer to the white people. But it was bullshit. Korean-speaking people, English-speaking Koreans gathered separately, American people gathered separately. . . . If we really are a minority, sadly, and being accused because of smells like kimchi, then we would really yearn to join the majority, their better culture. When it was like, the old days, it would be like that, because I would be ashamed of my being. Because my culture was not well treated. I would want to go to their culture [and be assimilated]. But now Korean culture is hot. Kimchi and bulgogi are rather sophisticated foods. It is a time when K-dramas or K-pop music is coming to the attention of other [non-Korean] kids. And I don't have anything to be blamed about. Rather, our people can gather together comfortably [and proudly]. The same is true with our children. The kids have nothing to be ashamed of, they even look down at the white kids, they aren't looked down upon.

I felt it was paradoxical that Kyung shared these thoughts in a European restaurant—not in a Korean or any other ethnic restaurant—where there were mostly white people around us. He indicated to me that the restaurant was the favorite place of white people in the area. In this place, he talked about racial equality and proud Korean-ness. Yet, his comments about racial segregation and the exclusive gatherings of Koreans and about "looking down" on white people, the majority group, reminded me of the warning of Paulo Freire, which is that persons who were once oppressed can become or want to become the oppressors:

> The oppressed suffer from the duality which has established itself in their innermost being. They discover that without freedom they cannot exist authentically. Yet, although they desire authentic existence, they fear it. They are at one and the same time themselves and the oppressor whose consciousness they have internalized. The conflict lies in the choice between being wholly themselves or being divided; between ejecting the oppressor within or not ejecting them; between human solidarity or alienation; between following prescriptions or having choices; between being spectators or actors; between acting or having the illusion of acting through the action of the oppressors; between speaking out or being silent, castrated in their power to create and re-create, in their power to transform the world. This is the tragic dilemma of the oppressed which their education must take into account.[17]

In other words, Korean immigrants, including Kyung, seem to be reproducing what they have felt in the past, such as marginalization, alienation, or oppression, and imposing it onto other people as if they are now socioeconomically changed and improved. I do not see in these Koreans any of Freire's "authentic being" or true Christian solidarity or social justice. Such attitudes and actions among Koreans demonstrate that religious ethics and Jesus's teachings, which have been taught in the church, are not applied in daily life.

Exclusionary practices should not be replicated by Koreans in the United States, which was once a foreign land to Korean immigrants, but is now a homeland to their descendants. Such exclusiveness and distorted self-esteems are also manifested in the education of children. Kyung expressed pride in the education fever and elitism among Koreans:

> In some ways, Korean people are highly competitive in education and it is a distinctive characteristic. It's characteristic. When Obama praised Korea's education fever, he gave confidence to Korean parents. And Korean parents in America are in fact very proud of how they raise their children. Because their grades and ranks prove it. People even say that, if there is a Korean student who is not successful in their studies, something's wrong with them. There will be pros and cons. But at least the advantage of it [the educational success of Korean students collectively] is that these kids can be proud of themselves. No matter where they go, they are confident.

---

17. Freire, *Pedagogy of the Oppressed*, 48.

Interestingly, of the several different responses I received from my interviewees about racism, only one respondent (Min) precisely presented the term *model minority* as a cultural phenomenon that describes the intersection of three major influences, which are Christian evangelism, Confucian morality, and racial stereotypes:

> I have my answer. In social work, a representative model looking at Asian youths is . . . well, what is the word I am looking for . . . the Asian role model. . . . If that's a role-model student . . . not a nerd. You know, Asian students are well behaving, following the rules, and Christians are diligent and obedient, right? They are good at studying, but the problem is that there are kids who don't fit in [such a category] exactly. I'm sorry to say that, but like my kid who doesn't study well. What is that word? Model minority. Right! Model minority. I think that is the intersection of Koreans [Korean American Christians]. Isn't that right? Mostly, yes, they attend church regularly, their first-generation immigrant parents also attend church regularly, and they are successful at school. Good kids. And the family maintains a social status quo [in the mainline society]. But there are children who do not fit in for sure. But those kids . . . deprivation and alienation they need to deal with . . . that's a huge problem. Some of the Asian kids who are drug addicts are getting worse than anyone else [anyone from other racial/ethnic groups]. They become hopeless. I think this is it as an intersection. There are many first-generation Korean parents who are going to church because of this.

Human life cannot always be adorned with success. Sometimes there are failures, frustrations, absurdities, controversies, and irreconcilable differences between us and family members or others who think differently from us. These are all useful building materials in developing the character of an individual, as discussed in the previous chapter, and they all play a role in building a person's own unique and solid house. Then, why are there always stories of wealthy families and successful children in the faith community? Rather, the church should be filled with stories about those who are broken, powerless, and sick and are healed by God's grace. But if the stories of failure are silenced in the church, or people are alienated from the community, and thus there are only stories of success and praise for their own members, is this a church? Is this an educational path that the church wants to press on with? This is not the church we want to dream of. This is not a faith community Jesus would ever imagine.

Considering the issue of elitism, the children's messages during my ethnographic research were coincidental, yet so elaborately fit into the theme of God's chosen people obeying God's way in a foreign land. The story of Ruth, a Gentile widow who obeyed her mother-in-law, followed her to Israel, and eventually was recorded in the glorious genealogy of Jesus, conforms well to the beliefs of the Confucian patriarchal order and filial piety. The story of Daniel in Babylonia, a boy who kept his faith in the lions' den, was also told in one service I attended, and the emphasis was on how we should live our lives faithfully and thoroughly to please God. These are, of course, engaging Bible stories anybody would enjoy. However, when such Bible teaching is combined with a Korean way of thinking, which consists of competitive elitism and a patriarchal hierarchy, it creates a trinitarian combination of Christian evangelism, Confucian hierarchy, and the model minority stereotype. Then it becomes a solid fortress of thought that is hard to break down.

According to Min Zhou and Susan Kim, even though parents seek to create better life conditions for their children, there are negative consequences to the mental and structural pressure to succeed found both at home and in society. Zhou and Kim note, "Tremendous pressure on both children and parents for school achievement can lead to intense intergenerational conflict, rebellious behavior, alienation from the networks that are supposed to assist them, and even withdrawal from formal schools. . . . Ironically, pressures and conflicts in a resourceful ethnic environment can also serve to fulfill parental expectations."[18] Likewise, Lisa Sun-Hee Park warns that "the model minority myth, and its accompanying disciplinary silence, is a central barrier for Asian Americans seeking to establish their social belonging."[19]

If the triad of oppressive cultural and religious elements I have noted become the collective values of Korean immigrant churches, if these churches do not foster faith formation for each generation and stick to the schooling-instructional paradigm, and if these churches emphasize success-driven faith and blessing, there will be no transformation of people into disciples of Christ. Second-generation children will inevitably feel a sense of divergence from the Korean community and eventually leave Korean congregations to find their own refuges that address their wounds and hopes.

18. Zhou and Kim, "Community Forces and Educational Achievement," 23.
19. Lisa Park, "Significance of the Model Minority Myth," 506.

Along with the crisis of the COVID-19 pandemic, the Atlanta shooting in March 2021 revealed the issue of anti-Asian racism that is deeply rooted in American culture. Korean immigrant churches can no longer avoid talking about racism. As Asians living in the US, and as disciples of Christ, we need to face the world with faith and discuss how to respond to such intersectional issues as race, gender, class, and climate change. Nathaniel D. West, professor and practitioner of Christian education, points out that religious education is about leading people to be engaged in public ministry and social change. He asserts, "The challenge and need is for the religious educator to be present with people in community, thereby showing God's presence."[20] Therefore, we need to raise our voices and work in solidarity against social injustice so that our children can live in a better world. I believe that the church should recognize this shared responsibility and that church education should play a practical role in helping people take it on.

Recently, in the *UM News*, I urged Korean immigrant churches to reconsider and strengthen their educational ministries. At the end of my essay I wrote,

> The moments of despair and anger that come to us today are not the end of us. Just as we have worked together to cultivate a new life in a foreign-but-not-foreign land, we are moving forward from the dark night to dawn. So I still dream of a day when second and coming generations of Asian American children freely claim their voice and purpose, find their ontological vocations with God's grace and vision and joyfully, confidently make their journey in the world. There is still a long way to go in this time of fear and hatred in the world. Yet, the day is coming. The day is coming.[21]

To sum up this chapter, through interviews and observations, I have identified four categories of current issues in the life and faith of Korean American immigrant congregations: (1) a family and community-oriented lifestyle, (2) aging congregations and a generation gap, (3) banking model education and a lack of faith formation efforts for all ages, and (4) the internalized racial stereotype of the model minority complex. I have confirmed that a Confucian patriarchal mindset, internalized racial stereotypes, and success-driven religious practices are still strong in the lives of first-generation Korean immigrant parents. At the same time, however, I also

---

20. West, "Educators as Public Ministry Leaders," 39.
21. Hwang, "Churches Must Nurture Younger Generations."

witnessed that members of aging communities are trying to transform their faith communities to meet the needs and desires of younger generations: Generation X and the early Millennials and their children—Generation Z and Alpha, or Shin Yi Se, the emerging new second-generation Korean Americans. In order not to repeat their shortcomings and wounds, they were trying to find a breakthrough by creating young family ministry initiatives.

In the following chapters, I will discuss theological and theoretical grounds for a new model of education. Specifically, theologies of childhood and children's education will be reviewed in relation to the Korean American church context. Then I will discuss developmental theories of faith and identity formation and offer an alternative framework.

Chapter 3

BECOMING LIKE CHILDREN

JINWOO

One day, Jinwoo's parents came to me and asked me some tough theological questions that had been raised by Jinwoo. Jinwoo was a fourth grader and a curious boy who asked a lot of questions, most of them silly. His parents often felt that they didn't know how to answer his questions. They were struggling with their own faith and having a hard time articulating it in adult language. The easiest answer for them to give Jinwoo to get them out of the situation was, "Why don't you go ask Pastor Heesung?" No matter what the questions were, Jinwoo's questions always made me perplexed, embarrassed, or amused. His questions were sometimes creative and sparkling, such as, "Why did God use mostly blue and green, but not pink, when creating the world?" Sometimes the questions were serious, deep, and realistically creative, like, "Why do good people still suffer?" Why aren't bad people judged or punished?" And, "What if Jesus returns to earth by the time I die and go to heaven, will the throne in heaven be empty or will Jesus be in both places, on earth and in heaven, at the same time?"

It was not easy to answer Jinwoo's questions. His questions sounded simple, but they often required a long explanation and conversation. So, my role was to listen to Jinwoo first, converse with him as often as possible, and grow with him during our time in the children's ministry. I do not think children always want to get answers to their questions. They just enjoy knowing that there is someone who is listening to their thoughts and willing to communicate with them, recognizing their curiosity and imagination. In fact, their free and creative questions invite me—or we adults—to reflect on God's mysteries. Rather than feeling the burden that I need to provide answers to children and their families, as a professional, I think it is important to enlighten parents that they do not need to feel like they have to be able to answer all their children's questions. Rather, they need to show their children their sincerity and faithfulness by living with love and care. Parents also need to know that they have the responsibility to nurture their children in faith as their children's primary educators. Thus, for me as a Christian educator, raising children in Christian faith and helping adults recognize the importance of childhood have been primary goals in my research and ministry.

UNLESS YOU BECOME LIKE A CHILD

> At that time the disciples came to Jesus and asked, "Who is the greatest in the kingdom of heaven?" Then he called a little child over to sit among the disciples, and said, "I assure you that if you don't turn your lives around and become like this little child, you will definitely not enter the kingdom of heaven. Those who humble themselves like this little child will be the greatest in the kingdom of heaven. Whoever welcomes one such child in my name welcomes me. (Matthew 18:1–5, CEB)

In this pericope from the Gospel of Matthew, the disciples are arguing about greatness in heaven. Given the situation of the Mediterranean world in the first century, with its male-centered patriarchal societies, the disciples' way of thinking reveals their social structure and their ambitions for upward mobility and success. They are concerned about their rank in heaven based on a worldly concept of honor and power. Then Jesus calls a child to him, puts this child in the disciples' midst, and challenges them to be like this child. In interpreting this passage, some scholars focus on the nature of a child, such as trust, dependency, or vulnerability.[1] Other scholars pay attention to the child's objective reality in the social context of the first century, as the weakest and the lowest in the patriarchal family structure.[2] Either

---

1. Berryman, *Children and the Theologians*, 185; Gundry-Volf, "Least and the Greatest," 41.

2. K. White, "'He Placed a Little Child'"; Grobbelaar, "Jesus and the Children"; Gundry, "Children in Mark." "Children do not denote innocence or purity. They were excluded from adult male society, powerless, without economic resources, vulnerable,

way, Jesus' response to the disciples is radical and subversive. He subverts the notion of greatness. Whether by resembling the character of children or by taking on their social position as vulnerable and powerless, the disciples, who are thinking about getting more power and status even after entering heaven, must engage with this radical call.[3]

Jerome Berryman, a Christian educator who is best known for his Godly Play approach, points out that "learning from children to become like children will mean becoming more curious, frank, hopeful, trusting, and eager to relate and communicate, and being full of vitality and imagination."[4] We need to keep this understanding in mind. In God's grace, we all, whether old or young, are the same. Children, as well as adults, have unique gifts to bring to the community. When Jesus said that the kingdom of God is for people like children, he meant that children should be fully respected for their worth and gifts. Adults often invite children to adult worship and force them to behave like adults, ignoring their agency and their implicit value. Such worship services imply that adults are the hosts and the controllers of the services, and the children are just guests and observers.

This text from Matthew is more challenging to put into practice in the context of Korean immigrant churches, where it is difficult for those with different languages and cultures to share a common worship experience. Even if the family worship service is offered without any language barriers, children's presence in the service is not often welcomed by the whole worshiping community. The children are often forced to sit up straight on adult-sized pews and to be quiet and sit still while adults worship and pray. Rather than providing a meaningful and inclusive worship experience for little children, the congregation is pleased that people of all generations are simply sitting together. Children will still feel and experience the atmosphere and wonder in the adult worship service. Yet, the community strongly desires to create more meaningful worship and education experiences for all, moving beyond the situation of simply sitting together during worship or having age-appropriate worship and education services for first

---

unpredictable, threatening, submissive . . . The Gospel has shown them to be endangered (chap. 2), hungry (14:21), sick (8:6; 9:2), demon-possessed (15:22; 17:18), and dead (9:18). Being a disciple means renouncing values of greatness and taking up the humble ways of dangerous children." Carter, "Gospel according to Matthew," 1778.

3. David H. Jensen argues that we need to pay attention to *both* the status and nature of children. Jensen, *Graced Vulnerability*, 126–28.

4. Berryman, *Children and the Theologians*, 185.

and second generations separately. Here, interpreting the previously cited Matthean text, David Jensen offers a significant insight about becoming like a child:

> What would becoming like a child resemble? The escape of Peter Pan? The wail of a baby? The curiosity of a preschooler? Drawing on a suggestive essay by Karl Rahner, I suggest that becoming like a child implies our partnership with God, in frank admission of the vulnerability and brokenness of human life. To become like a child, in this sense, is to become who we already are—the full inheritors of God's blessing and election of us, valued not for who will become, but for whose we already are. . . . Rahner's account is fundamentally relational. Children, from the beginning, are aware of human relationality in the caress of loving arms and the soothing notes of a lullaby. To submit to the power of life in relation (not death and abuse), to recognize that we are not alone, is to embrace mystery.[5]

Jansen's wisdom that being like a child means recognizing the weakness and brokenness of life and walking with God and others provides a clue as to what we should do in our churches. In these relational communities, both adults and children should experience life, hope, and growth in God's forgiving love and grace.

CHILDREN AS ALREADY FULLY HUMAN AND THEOLOGIANS IN THEIR OWN WAYS

In her book *Welcoming Children: A Practical Theology of Childhood*, practical theologian Joyce Ann Mercer asserts that, from the time they are born, children are "already fully human, whole-yet-broken people."[6] According to Mercer, the perspective that considers children as less important or less developed beings leads to indifference and lack of care. Such a prevalent perspective shows that we have been ignoring an important part of God's presence in our midst by ignoring the value and roles of the children among us.[7] Mercer claims that they are fully human but still developing. This "in-progress" status does not imply that they are less human. God created human beings in God's own image, so children already bear the full

---

5. Jensen, *Graced Vulnerability*, 127, 129.
6. Mercer, *Welcoming Children*, 251.
7. Berryman, *Becoming Like a Child*, 919.

image of God.[8] In the very beginning, "God created humanity in God's own image, in the divine image God created them, male and female God created them."[9] Every human being has been created by God in God's image, regardless of gender, class, race, or any circumstances. This notion applies to every child on the planet, whether he or she is physically or emotionally mature, "legal or illegal, documented or undocumented, citizen or alien."[10] All children are precious children of God.

Children, who are "fully alive, fully present, fully endowed with promise in God's world," recognize God and expand their experience of God in their own ways.[11] One cannot say that they are not aware of the divine presence in and around them simply because they do not process it or articulate it logically. Berryman argues, "Sometimes adults greatly underestimate children's experience of God and the kind of theological thought they are capable of when they have appropriate materials and informed adults to work with them."[12] We must respect the mystery of life and the grace of God in children's experiences and questions. In the ways of children, children's creativity and curiosity guide them to understand themselves, God, and the world. According to Christian educator Elizabeth Caldwell, "The chance to wonder about the Bible as they wander through their life is essential for a child's spiritual formation, for developing a language of faith."[13] In the process of working with children, adults learn as much as children do.[14] Respecting children's ways of learning and doing theology opens the way for adults to become like children.

DEFINITIONS OF FAITH AND RELIGIOUS EDUCATION FOR CHILDREN

With the theological understanding of children provided in the previous section, my attention turns to the next phase: What do we want to teach children about faith? What do adults and children want to learn about, and how can they grow together? As Mercer points out, "Education into this

---

8. Mercer, *Welcoming Children*, 252; Miller-McLemore, *Let the Children Come*, 138.
9. Genesis 1:27, CEB.
10. Berryman, *Becoming Like a Child*, 622; Groody, "Crossing the Divide," 639.
11. Jensen, *Graced Vulnerability*, 122.
12. Berryman, *Children and the Theologians*, 5.
13. Caldwell, *I Wonder*, ix.
14. Berryman, *Children and the Theologians*, 7–8; Jensen, *Graced Vulnerability*, 123.

Christian identity is hardly politically neutral, as Freire understood well."[15] In other words, faith and the goals of education that a church defines are so important that they will determine the future direction of the faith community and children's lives.

Experiencing the Bible with Children by Christian educator Dorothy Jean Furnish offers great insight into how to experience the Bible as a living story and to do theology with children. Furnish writes, "The goal of Bible study with children is to open the Bible for them in such a way that they are able to experience the Bible content and discover meaning for their present lives, while keeping open the possibility of future learning and meanings."[16] Her suggestion of understanding the Bible as a "now" event is an especially important concept.[17] The Bible is not simply old stories or a documentary of history and people. Rather, the Bible should be considered an active event that is relevant to our lives. Furnish also makes an important point about maintaining openness to various possible interpretations of biblical passages over one's lifespan. She writes, "Although the Bible is a timeless document, it is understood differently at different times."[18] When children interact with friends who have different understandings of the Bible or who have different faith traditions, they get frustrated or confused by perspectives that are different from those presented in their own faith community. It is important to help children respect and honor diversity. For traveling on the journey of faith with children, Furnish introduces various methods—such as playing games, telling stories, painting, and listening to and creating music—through which children can engage with and experience the Bible. I believe it is important to provide a space for children to express and respond to what they feel, understand, or are frustrated about. As Furnish suggests, "When children are asked to express their feelings and ideas, care should be taken that their comments not be manipulated so as to please the teacher."[19]

Some years ago, I was at a retreat for fifty upper elementary children. The speaker asked the children some questions related to the Bible and said, "If you do not know the answer, remember that 85 percent of the right answer will be Jesus." Back then, I didn't realize how terrible this statement

---

15. Mercer, *Welcoming Children*, 168.
16. Furnish, *Experiencing the Bible*, 7.
17. Furnish, *Experiencing the Bible*, 25.
18. Furnish, *Experiencing the Bible*, 35.
19. Furnish, *Experiencing the Bible*, 80.

was. The retreat was full of laughter and of children saying the correct answer, which was "Jesus." However, this educational method manipulated and pushed children to say the "correct" answer, regardless of their understanding or faith. We need to wait for children to find their own personal meanings, whether they are correct ones according to given knowledge or not. We need to let them respond using their own creativity. We need to encourage children to wonder and to find the answers to their own situations and problems.

The problem with churches in the twenty-first century, especially Korean immigrant churches, is, as mentioned in the introduction, that churches have taught an irrelevant gospel that does not consider the current situation. Sarah Shin, a campus minister and the author of *Beyond Colorblind: Redeeming our Ethnic Journey*, argues,

> Our lack of ethnic identity understanding for ourselves and those around us led to a proclamation of a gospel that is irrelevant or powerless in addressing real aches, pains, and questions. Racially and culturally unaware witness and involvement in our communities caused distrust; we sometimes did more harm than good and pushed people away from us—away from opportunities to hear the gospel and away from trusting Jesus. What resulted was and is a distant and often irrelevant, unaffected church. . . . Colorblindness mutes Christian voices and thoughts from speaking into ethnic brokenness.[20]

Written from the perspective of evangelical faith, Shin's book does not address current cultural controversies, such as the concerns of interfaith dialogue or LGBTQIA+ people of faith. Yet this book still has significance in that it links the teachings of the church with the problems of racism and deals with feminism and liberation from an Asian cultural background. Shin offers practical ways to engage in social conversations for racial reconciliation in faith communities, especially in the setting of campus ministry. Then, what is faith for first-generation immigrants living in a foreign land and for second-generation children who still live as strangers in their homeland? To overcome the irrelevant and ineffective gospel that Shin mentioned, we should consider the whole of church education and think about alternative approaches. As a first step in this process, I will define what faith and religious education are.

---

20. Shin, *Beyond Colorblind*, 7.

Theologian and educator James Fowler, in his article "Strength for the Journey: Early Childhood Development in Selfhood and Faith," describes faith as a process of constructively understanding the relationship between oneself and ultimate existence, the world, and others.[21] Applying this understanding in relation to people's faith-driven public responsibility, religious educator Gabriele Klappenecker argues that faith is an ongoing endeavor to discover and develop the relationships that give meaning to oneself and to public life in an age of diversity.[22] In the sense that children build up positive emotions and meanings while growing psychologically and spiritually in relation to themselves and others, I define *faith* for children as a process of gathering meaning-blocks and of building a house of being in companionship with God and others. The blocks may be strong because of positive experiences and affirmation, or weak because of broken materials caused by wounds and frustrations. It is through the grace of God that all these things—both strong and broken blocks—can be combined to form a house of being.

In his book, *Teaching the Way of Jesus*, religious educator Jack Seymour emphasizes that "education 'prophetically' calls a people back to their deepest and most important values. Education helps contemporary people to 'artistically' connect current experience with these values. Therefore, educators examine the variety of social procedures that teach, their interrelationships, and their outcomes."[23] This definition of *education*, which speaks of finding the most important meanings in relation to oneself and the world is in line with the direction I am aiming for religious education for children to go. Therefore, it is the role of religious education to help children acquire helpful meaning-blocks from the beginning of their lives onward and to repair and connect the broken parts of their houses of being in the midst of their various experiences while growing up. In such education, as Mercer points out, "Children learn not simply in order to 'have information' in their heads. In this kind of education children learn

---

21. "Faith also involves an evolving construction of a sense of relatedness to others and to an ultimate environment. The ultimate environment is symbolized in our culture, and in most others, by some kind of God-representation, some sort of symbol or image of an ultimate being or an ultimate reality. Faith, in addition to a sense of relatedness to ultimate being or ultimate reality, includes a sense of relatedness to the world, the neighbor, [and] the self, in light of that ultimate relatedness." J. Fowler, "Strength for the Journey," 3.

22. Klappenecker, "Development of Public Responsibility," 48.

23. Seymour, *Teaching the Way of Jesus*, 44.

to constitute (and 'be constituted into') a way of life and an identity as persons participating in the kin-dom of God."[24] Children and adults together expand and develop the community of faith through active participation and dialogue with one another and the world. I will further elaborate on this metaphor of meaning-blocks and a house of being for a developmental understanding of childhood in the next chapter.

RAISING CHILDREN AS A RELIGIOUS PRACTICE OF A COMMUNITY

Children bear diverse and creative possibilities for cultivating a better society and transforming the world. Children, simply by being children, provide insights into understanding God. As the body of Christ, we, the faith community, are called to recognize children as valuable gifts and as divine agents of God.[25] Therefore, it is important to understand the value of children and the role of religious education for the sake of the entire faith community, as well as for children themselves.

Raising children, helping children build a sturdy house of being, is not just the responsibility of their biological parents. A supportive community and a social support system are absolutely necessary for children as well as for their parents. We are called to practice God's love and stewardship in a communal journey of raising children for a better future.[26] Therefore, church education ministries should help young parents ensure that faith education is done at home as an initial step toward a lifelong faith journey. Practical theologian Pamela Couture, in her book *Seeing Children, Seeing God*, expands the responsibility for raising children beyond families and local congregations to communities beyond the church. Needless to say, every child deserves a loving and caring environment, emotionally and financially as well as spiritually. Yet, there are so many children who don't receive such care. Couture calls our attention specifically to children living in poverty. Whether children are suffering from "material poverty [or] the poverty of tenuous connections," they should be in our prayers and

---

24. Mercer, *Welcoming Children*, 168–69. Mercer replaces the word *kingdom*, which is male-centered and imperialistic, with the term *kin-dom*. Joining the Christian feminist conversation, I will make the same substitution. Stevens, "We Are Family."

25. Caldwell, *God's Big Table*, 109.

26. Mercer, *Welcoming Children*, 205. See also Fretheim, "'God Was with the Boy,'" 276.

subjects of our actions.²⁷ According to Couture, the teachings of families and communities are "words of liberation when they result in practices that contribute to the resilience of children and those who care for them . . . a resilience that is tenacious because it arises from God's grace."²⁸ The God of grace "enacts justice for orphans and widows, and he loves immigrants, giving them food and clothing."²⁹ Following God's law and Jesus's example in our actions for little ones is a crucial responsibility for us as Christ's disciples. Couture also believes, on the foundation of God's law, that every child has the fundamental and equal right to be connected to the "social ecology, . . . , such as local communities, governments, and cultural identities, that provide for the needs of the child for survival, development, and flourishing."³⁰ This reminds us that church education must be linked to all social systems in order to provide life and faith for children inside and outside of the church community.

Children in church communities can also participate in making a better world for their peers in the world. For example, I used to have a mission project in my children's ministry. It involved a couple of weeks of teaching on world poverty and some plans for action during Lent, for example, a campaign of collecting goods and engaging in intercessory prayers for children in our area and the adult mission team. It was one of the most powerful ministry experiences those involved had that strengthened children's relationships with God and others. Both children and adults took the next step on their faith journey by acting out what they had learned through the mission project and from each other. Through such community experiences, I wanted children to learn that faith is not something to own but a verb to practice. I hoped that adults would realize the sacred value of children's existence through engaging in a mission project with young children. I hoped that children and adults could gather more constructive meaning-blocks. So, I hoped Jinwoo's questions would find some answers.

Children's questions don't stop when they go home from church. As they experience the world beyond their relationships with their families and God, their curiosity and questions expand. Especially during the coronavirus pandemic, children have asked us challenging questions. Why did

27. Couture, *Seeing Children, Seeing God*, 14.
28. Couture, *Seeing Children, Seeing God*, 16.
29. Deuteronomy 10:18, CEB.
30. Couture, *Seeing Children, Seeing God*, 43.

God make the coronavirus? Will God protect us from the virus?[31] Why do some people call it the Chinese virus?[32] Why do people hate and kill people of color? Why did the police kill Georgy Floyd?[33] Why did the white man shoot at Asian women in Atlanta?[34] Rather than relying on what they experienced during their childhoods, adults should understand and deal with children's questions today within the twenty-first-century sociocultural context. My next chapter will explore theories of children's faith and identity formation, and I will present a new religious education framework for the Shin Yi Se, the new generation of children.

---

31. In a study conducted by the University of Chicago Divinity School and The Associated Press-NORC Center for Public Affairs Research, "More than half of the respondents polled also said they believed God would protect them from infection. Broken down by affiliation, 67% of white Evangelical Christians agreed with that statement, compared to 53% of other Americans who believe in God." H. Fowler, "'God Will Protect Me.'"

32. Bostock, "Trump's Tweet about a 'Chinese Virus.'"

33. B. Parks, "Floyd's Death Was 'Murder'"; Hill et al., "Floyd Was Killed in Police Custody."

34. Lynch and Volcovici, "Atlanta Shooting Was Racially Motivated."

Chapter 4

HOW DO THEY GROW UP?

ALICE

ALICE WAS THREE-AND-A-HALF YEARS old at the time and always had a good attitude. She was accustomed to sitting on an adult-sized chair and sat quietly during the worship service for the elementary kids—there was no separate worship or activity for preschoolers—until the adults' worship service was over. She was not talkative; she just said a little bit when she wanted to say something. When she was drawing and coloring, she was very good at connecting dots and coloring inside the lines. At first I thought she was just more mature than her peers and somehow very good at self-control. However, when she approached me during the worship service to point out that the child sitting on the chair next to her was not behaving well, I was a bit surprised. She came to me to report the same boy three times during that service. I became worried about her and the discipline practices in her home. Maybe she was naturally exacting and self-controlled, but, if her parents and grandparents were disciplining her too strictly, it was possible that she was growing up under great pressure to be a perfectionist.

It is not easy to open up a conversation about children's behavior with their parents, especially in a church setting where most people have a Korean cultural background. In Korea, people usually don't talk about painful or shameful subjects with others outside their families. So, I began my conversation with Alice's parents by offering praise for how well Alice had done over the weeks I had observed her, and I carefully brought up the issue of her exacting attitude toward herself and others. They seemed to be okay with her manner at home. In fact, her mother was happy to hear that she was behaving well. They didn't consider her behavior an issue. Because Alice was the first child in their family and extended families, they seemed to think her attitude as a first daughter was appropriate. I worried, however, that Alice might have been caught up in her sense of responsibility as a first daughter and the need to behave nicely and maintain her manners. Then, at the end of our conversation about my careful observation of her behavior, her father insisted, "She's still three and a half. What does she know? She's too young to know anything." With these statements, the conversation ended. I was taken aback by the father's understanding of children's growth and cognitive development. I was also embarrassed that I was not knowledgeable enough to tell Alice's parents how a typical three- to four-year-old child would feel and think.

In the past, people often thought of children as objects that needed adults' guidance and nurture. However, recent studies approach children as independent agents on their own spiritual journeys.[1] Children, by simply being children, provide insights for understanding God and the world. In her book *Welcoming Children*, Joyce Ann Mercer emphasizes why the faith community should recognize children as divine gifts:

> When we look to children, when we know them well enough and care for them deeply enough to welcome them, then we get the chance to know some things about God and to come to know God differently than might otherwise occur. If welcoming a child is a way to welcome God, then perhaps there is something about God that is as messy, playful, noisy, active, spontaneous, restless, and unpredictable as that which one encounters in welcoming a child. Maybe by learning to truly welcome even the most restless of children, for instance, I thereby learn to welcome God's restlessness as an aspect of God's being that I might otherwise not recognize or care to encounter.[2]

This childlike aspect of the divine is the image of God that we have lost. Jerome Berryman also points out the sacred value of children as theologians.[3] It is children who remind us of God's image, of God's presence, and of the divine care that is among us. They inspire stubborn adults with diverse and creative possibilities for thriving together in the world. I wish I

---

1. See Campen, *Holy Work with Children*.
2. Mercer, *Welcoming Children*, 262.
3. Berryman, *Children and the Theologians*, 177.

could have shared these ideas with Alice's parents back then. I wish I could continue to observe Alice's growth as she navigates through childhood and discovers herself, her family, others, and God.

BUILDING WITH MEANING-BLOCKS: A MODIFIED BIOECOLOGICAL MODEL OF CHILD DEVELOPMENT

Current child development theories, most of which have been produced by white male scholars, assert that children at each phase of life have a task to achieve for development, and whether a child succeeds or fails at that task determines whether the child will develop enough to become a mature adult. Even though there is a possibility of revisiting previous stages and rebuilding the life skills of those stages, such theories are still deeply tied to a sequential structure.[4] In the structure of a life ladder, if one does not complete the mission at each stage successfully, it is difficult to have healthy psychosocial growth. The failures or negative results from the previous stages cast a shadow over one's life, hindering one's walk through the next stage. Such theories of development based on the dichotomous thinking of success versus failure do not adequately explain the cognitive and thought development of people of color, especially Asians. Besides, we often dismiss children as immature and ignorant. We tend to emphasize that a mature adult is a person who thinks metaphysically and creates relationships based on the values of capitalism, aiming only for financially beneficial relationships. As I said in the last chapter, we need to see the divinity in children and recover their curiosity, creativity, and open attitudes toward God and the world.

Therefore, the house of being that I am presenting is built with all the failures and successes of life. Rather than having sequentially accumulated negative factors in development, a child might build a house of meaning with both life-giving and confusing or misleading blocks. Any part of the house with broken or misshapen building blocks will be vulnerable to inner and outer dangers. Yet, life is full of dilemmas and paradoxes anyway. As "already fully human, whole-yet-broken people," we, the children of God, can grow up carrying both life-giving and life-deterring elements together.[5] God embraces us, not because we are perfect and successful, but because we are just the way we are, with brokenness, ironies, and dilemmas.

4. Yust, *Real Kids, Real Faith*, 11.
5. Mercer, *Welcoming Children*, 251.

And God's divine intervention and transformation can patch up or cover up the broken blocks of a person.

With assistance from adults or peers, a child's house of life can be mended, strengthened, and expanded (figure 7). In this model of a house of being, human development does not occur in isolation. Rather, it stimulates communal and interactive growth.[6] The scaffolding for the house of being is for temporary support. Once the building or fixing process is completed, the scaffolding will be gradually taken away.[7] Based on careful observation and interactions with a child, the pieces of the child's scaffolding should be adjusted. Cynthia Jones Neal explains, "When we scaffold, focusing on our learners' levels of understanding, building on their strengths, using their misunderstandings to adjust our level of support, our learners will begin the process of creating knowledge and meaning for themselves."[8] I believe this process is something we should focus on in children's education. Rather than focusing on giving children tasks and rewarding them for achievements, we should provide children with enough space—safe and free space—to follow their curiosity and to create their own meanings.

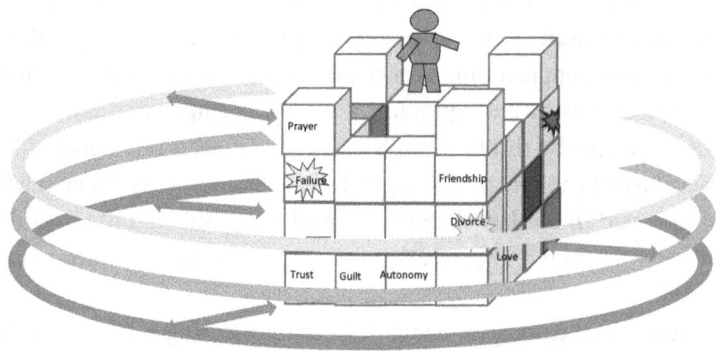

Figure 7. Scaffolding for a child's house of being

The bioecological system theory of Urie Bronfenbrenner, a Russian-born American psychologist and a co-founder of the national Head Start program, goes along with the process of finding meaning in all aspects of life and of forming one's own identity. This theory emphasizes organic growth and expansion in various social interrelationships. The social elements that

6. Neal, "Power of Vygotsky," 125.
7. Neal, "Power of Vygotsky," 133.
8. Neal, "Power of Vygotsky," 136.

help a child build a strong house of meaning are diverse and multilayered. Bronfenbrenner's bioecological model, based on Lev Vygotsky's theory, includes multiple levels of environments that affect the development of an individual child.[9] Bronfenbrenner's original ecological model had four nested systems: the microsystem, mesosystem, exosystem, and macrosystem; later, he added a time-related system, the chronosystem, and renamed his theory the bioecological model of human development.[10] Bronfenbrenner argues that personal development takes place through interacting with these five environmental systems.[11] No system exists in isolation or gradually disappears, like the scaffolding in Vygotsky's theory, but each interacts with and influences the other systems and is transformed organically.[12]

First, in Bronfenbrenner's theory, the microsystem is the environment that is the closest to and has the most direct impact on the individual child. It includes the influences of family members and of relationships in a daycare or school, which result in particular "behaviors, such as dependence or independence and cooperation or competition."[13] The second level is the mesosystem. This level is characterized by a combination of two or more microsystems, such as home and daycare, home and church, or family and neighbors, and no structure or element is independently present, but all are interrelated.[14] The third level, the exosystem, extends beyond the child's immediate environment, but it still has a significant link to the development of an individual. This system includes parents' workplaces and community services.[15] The fourth circle is the macrosystem. This system includes sociocultural customs, values, and laws that affect an individual. Fifth, the chronosystem refers to social and historical changes that occur

---

9. Russian education theorist Lev Vygotsky points out that human development occurs in interaction with cultural and historical factors. Unlike Jean Piaget, who focused on an individual child's cognitive development, Vygotsky insisted that social and cognitive development are intertwined and build on each other. Mooney, *Theories of Childhood*, 100.

10. Gardiner and Kosmitzky, *Lives across Cultures*, 23.

11. Gardiner and Kosmitzky, *Lives across Cultures*, 21–22.

12. Stewart, *Supporting Refugee Children*, 16. Montero points out, "Moving outward, Bronfenbrenner argued that the individual is also influenced, but to a lesser extent, by those relationships occurring in more distant settings, such as a neighborhood peer group (mesosystem), through teacher professional development (exosystem), and through societal cultural attitudes (macrosystem)." Montero, "Standing #WithRefugees," 124.

13. Gardiner and Kosmitzky, *Lives across Cultures*, 21–22.

14. Gardiner and Kosmitzky, *Lives across Cultures*, 21–22.

15. Gardiner and Kosmitzky, *Lives across Cultures*, 24.

during the growth of the individual child.[16] For example, the sociocultural events of the twenty-first century included in figure 3 (chapter 1), such as K-pop culture and the immigration policies of the Trump administration, are influential factors in the macrosystem and the chronosystem of Korean American children.

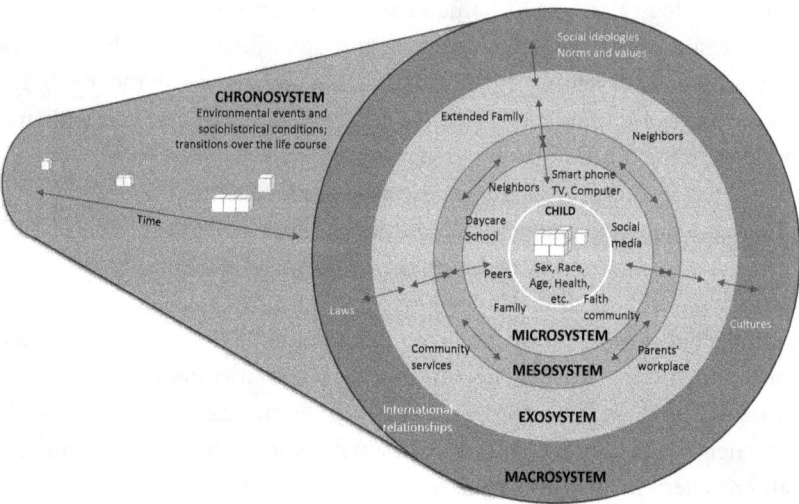

Figure 8. Bronfenbrenner's bioecological model of human development, modified[17]

Social and educational researcher Brian O'Neill, in his article "Ecological Perspectives and Children's Use of the Internet: Exploring Micro to Macro Level Analysis," applies Bronfenbrenner's theory specifically to the development of technology and children's use of electronic devices and the internet.[18] These are obviously emerging influential factors in children's lives today. While Bronfenbrenner's original theory located the influence of mass media in the exosystem, O'Neill claims that personal devices, such as smartphones and e-book reading devices, should be located in the microsystem since they are having a growing impact on children's lives and development in the twenty-first century. Hence, figure 8, which is based on Bronfenbrenner's bioecological model of human development, reflects my concept of collecting building blocks, along with O'Neill's suggestion of the

16. Gardiner and Kosmitzky, *Lives across Cultures*, 25.

17. O'Neill, "Ecological Perspectives," 40; Gardiner and Kosmitzki, *Lives across Cultures*, 24; Gardiner, *Lives across Cultures*, 15.

18. O'Neill, "Ecological Perspectives," 32–53.

influence of technology on Gen Z and Gen Alpha. I argue that every child is working to make meaning within their dynamic cultural reality. That meaning is profoundly influenced by parental figures and those closest to a child, yet the sphere of influence becomes larger as a child grows in relationship to church and school peers, neighbors, and media influences. We need to affirm children as meaning makers and realize that development is influenced by personal growth and by the environments that surround and influence a child.

Most developmental theories understand race as merely a personal trait, not as an influencing factor in child development. In other words, there is no consideration of how the identities of ethnic minority children who are growing up in white mainstream society develop in the midst of their sociocultural interactions. Grace Ji-Sun Kim's argument reveals how important race is in shaping a person's identity:

> Nonwhite immigrants can achieve cultural assimilation (adoption of American lifestyle), but structural assimilation (equal life-chances) is difficult to achieve as many see race as a permanently damaging factor. For example, second- or third-generation Asian Americans are often easily acculturated but it is difficult for them to be assimilated into American society on an equal basis because of their race; they will never be included as the dominant group of the "norm" in society. Race is a fundamental determinant of marginality for Asian Americans, for African Americans, Native Americans, and Hispanic Americans. Race trumps culture, as race is written on people's faces and skin, while their history and culture are not.[19]

In the field of development theory, there is only a small number of scholars who deal with racial identity formation. Among them, Jean Kim is one of a very few who deals with the Asian identity formation process. Until recently, the general direction and theoretical flow of racial/ethnic development theories reflected people's hope to assimilate into the mainstream white society. However, as noted in chapter 1, the racial and ethnic makeup of this society is changing rapidly, and soon white Americans will be a numerical minority, in fact, one of the minorities.[20] We must now focus on creatively claiming and affirming Asian physical features and identities in our rapidly changing American society, which is no longer so white.

---

19. G. J. Kim, *Embracing the Other*, 42; J. Y. Lee, *Marginality*, 34–35.
20. Hong, *Minor Feelings*, 72.

ASIAN AMERICAN IDENTITY DEVELOPMENT THEORY

Jean Kim, a Korean American scholar in education and identity development theory, argues that "Asian people's view of themselves (the private self) is primarily influenced by what other people (the public), and particularly what a specific group of people (the collective) think of them."[21] Identity formation is therefore a more complex process for Asians than for white Americans, and social, political, and cultural influences play a role.[22] Jean Kim's theory is one of the most prominent racial identity development theories for Asian Americans. She first developed her theory in the 1980s and revised it in the early 2000s. Over time, studies focused specifically on ethnic identity have been conducted, but her theory is still foundational and prominent. She describes Asian American identity development as consisting of five stages: ethnic awareness, white identification, awakening to social political consciousness, redirection to Asian American consciousness, and incorporation.[23] These five stages progress in order, but do not move from one into another linearly or automatically. In some cases, one may get stuck in a stage, not making any progress.[24]

At home, second-generation Korean American children are exposed to the Korean language, and they eat Korean food and watch Korean TV programs. In this way, they naturally come to understand that they have a Korean heritage. Experiences like these are helpful for Asian American children to feel a sense of security and to develop a positive image of their own ethnicity. The next stages of identity development typically begin when these children start attending an American school. Students in this period actively or passively seek to assimilate into the white mainstream culture. As long as they believe that they can fully assimilate into white society, regardless of age, Asian Americans remain at this stage, not moving forward.[25]

Yet, some Asian Americans shift their worldview and begin to look at the problem of social-structural racism. They "realize that regardless of what they achieve, they will never be fully accepted into the dominant

---

21. J. Kim, "Asian American Identity Development Theory," 67–68.
22. G. S. Kim, "Asian North American Youth," 206.
23. J. Kim, "Asian American Identity Development Theory," 72–81.
24. J. Kim, "Asian American Identity Development Theory," 72.
25. J. Kim, "Asian American Identity Development Theory," 76.

society as long as White racism exists."[26] Such a realization eventually leads them to navigate and reaffirm their identity as Asian Americans. According to Jean Kim, "The ego identity of Asian Americans at this stage is centered on being an Asian American, which entails knowing they belong here, having a clear political understanding of what it means to be Asian American in this society, and no longer seeing themselves as misfits."[27] Finally, Asian Americans strive for incorporation, which means having "confidence in one's own Asian American identity."[28] In this stage, an Asian American has the ability to engage in mutual communication with people of other races without losing his or her identity and confidence as an Asian American.

Jean Kim notes that she developed this theory by studying 1.5-plus generations and, therefore, it is more appropriate for them than for first-generation immigrants. She points out that first-generation immigrants who came to the United States as adults experience less psychological impact from racism than children of later generations who grow up with it. She also suggests that the cases of interracial and interreligious families should be considered for the further development of her theory, since her research does not address the development of children who have been born into interracial marriages.[29] Indeed, her suggestion is an appropriate and urgent challenge for further studies, considering that the demographics of Gen Z and Gen Alpha are more multicultural, multi-religious, and interracial. Therefore, my vision for my research is to help all children, as well as Asian American children, interact with various people and cultures in the world with confidence without being ashamed or confused about their identities.

I have claimed that children are capable of making meaning in relation to their environments. Regardless of their race, gender, or age, children need to be included in the lives of their faith communities.[30] Adults are responsible for providing a scaffolding for children's journey of meaning making. Now, let's explore how we adults can provide a scaffolding and a liberating space for Shin Yi Se children.

---

26. J. Kim, "Asian American Identity Development Theory," 78.
27. J. Kim, "Asian American Identity Development Theory," 79.
28. J. Kim, "Asian American Identity Development Theory," 80.
29. J. Kim, "Asian American Identity Development Theory," 84.
30. Campen, *Holy Work with Children*, 7, 13.

PUTTING IT TOGETHER: SOK PRACTICE FOR KOREAN AMERICAN CHILDREN

A child collects his or her own building blocks and builds a house of being. The broken parts of the blocks are also used as tools for building the house, yet through interaction with others, the child may repair the broken pieces. For this metaphor, I gained insight from the "temples of meaning" that Jack Seymour, Margaret Ann Crain, and Joseph Crockett describe: "Metaphorically, we dwell in personal 'temples of meaning.' Our temples are vital to our existence. They provide support and protection. They are always under construction or reconstruction."[31] These three educators go on to explain, "Humans also discover meanings as they connect personal meanings to meanings that are part of their cultures. Cultures provide shared symbols, a language, and expectations that form the context in which one learns. Persons who are part of a culture other than the dominant one encounter the power of community early in life."[32] Finding one's own voice, meaning, and purpose in life is a complex task, regardless of ethnicity, class, gender, or any other categories of identity. Yet, developing healthy identities can be a more challenging process for those who are dealing with nondominant values and cultures. My conviction after reviewing major developmental theories of childhood is that it is not solely the work of individuals to figure out their own voices and purposes in life. Rather, it is the responsibility of a child's parents and community, along with the child, so that the child can navigate through the meanings of his or her own life and grow up as an integrated and faithful being. Therefore, it is our responsibility as religious educators to help children gain more constructive building blocks through their personal and social interactions and to help them discover paint and glue (God's grace) to bring together the strong and poor blocks as they build up their own houses of life.

For this work, family fellowship can be a key to building safe spaces at the level of the microsystem for emerging new second-generation Korean American children. I suggested in the introduction to this book that the central point of intersection of Korean American Christians' three heritages is the practice of building meaningful relationships. Family fellowship is a way to build those relationships. It can be called by other names, such as "table fellowship" or "*sok*," which, in Korean church practice, means "a

---

31. Seymour, Crain, and Crockett, *Educating Christians*, 23.
32. Seymour, Crain, and Crockett, *Educating Christians*, 23–25.

small group gathering." Sharon Kim, in her book *A Faith of Our Own: Second-Generation Spirituality in Korean American Churches*, also discusses the important role of small group worship and fellowship among Korean American Christians, using the term *kuyok yabae*, meaning "regional Bible study and worship."[33] Although the use of terms can vary depending on the preferences of a congregation, the core concept and practice is the same as table fellowship. Yet, these fellowship gatherings are usually centered around adult members. I will continue using the word *sok* in this work in order to indicate my focus on children and the use of this community practice as an important way to support their faith and identity development.

In Korean-Chinese etymology, there are a couple of words that mean "family." Generally, *ga-jok* (가족, 家族) refers to "a legal and biological family unit." Another word is *sik-goo* (식구, 食口), which means "those who eat meals together." As a family, eating meals together means sharing physical and spiritual nutrition together. Although the word *sik-goo* is generally used for biological family members, it is also widely used to describe close members of a group or the members of a sok or congregation. In other words, Koreans generally say *sok sik-goo*, not *sok ga-jok*, and *kyohwe* ("church") *sik-goo*, not *kyohwe ga-jok*. This choice of words points to a specific cohesion in faith among those who share meals as well as life stories.

When families gather in a place, usually in the home of a family member, they begin the gathering with a meal or some desserts. Bible study and prayer follow. During the adults' Bible study, one or two adults volunteer to lead children's activities. For the closing prayer, all members, including the children, gather around and pray together and bless each other. A pastoral staff person assigns an older (or trained) church member as the group leader to organize these meetings and discussions. The pastor often makes a circuit to each sok to see if it is functioning well as members share their lives and faith with one another. When sok families gather weekly or bi-weekly, children also have a chance to mingle with other children. Sok meetings provide a great opportunity for children to interact with other children as well as adults in a family-friendly setting, with mostly ethnic food, culture, and language. Here lies the scaffolding for a child's development, since this type of gathering offers a chance to affirm positive strengths such as love, trust, and identity.

The principle of small groups can also be found in the Wesleyan tradition. The early Methodist movement set up three types of small groups in

33. S. Kim, *Faith of Our Own*, 320–21; Kim-Cragg, *Interdependence*, loc. 601–7 of 5054.

addition to regular church attendance as ways for members to help one another grow as disciples of Christ; these groups were called society meetings, class meetings, and band meetings.[34] The class meeting had a similar size and concept as family fellowship or sok gatherings in Korean church practice, which consist of around five families. Such a meeting functions as a small group unit for weekly Bible study or simply for fellowship. In any case, the practice of sok, or the class meeting, has been a great way to reach out to people and to bring them together in the Korean/Korean American context.

God's Big Table: Nurturing Children in a Diverse World, written by professor of religious education Elizabeth Caldwell, strengthens my conviction about the practice of sok. This book provides specific guidelines for parents and teachers to help children grow more faithfully and inclusively in a diverse world. Caldwell introduces aspects of the lives of children who do not fit the norms, such as different religious and racial backgrounds, same-sex parents, and the different learning processes that come with ADD/ADHD or autism. By including this wide range of differences, a faith community can be a truly beautiful and big table of sharing in God. Caldwell first provides some examples of biblical interpretation to deal with real questions of diversity in context, such as issues of different faiths, races, and gender relationships. Then, along with narratives for each case, she offers steps and guidelines to extend the table of fellowship. With a healthy understanding of one's own foundation, one can grow in faith within a faith community that works to transform the world. When families can bring rich and healthy conversations about social, racial, and religious issues to their tables as part of the process of "homemaking," they encourage the spiritual growth of the faith community as well as of individuals.[35]

Caldwell's suggestions are still challenging for local congregations, especially for Korean immigrant communities. To preserve ethnic traditions and faith in the midst of cultural pluralism, immigrant churches in general have become more exclusive and conservative. Within such communities, which put most of their energy and interest into preserving their theological understandings as well as their ethnic identity, the issues that Caldwell raises have been often neglected. There are even some parents who avoid

---

34. Iovino, "Disciples Making Disciples."

35. Caldwell defines *homemaking* as "creating a safe and intimate environment where the meanings that are deepest to ourselves can be shared and where we come to know what it means to live in the family named Christian." Caldwell, *God's Big Table*, 20.

any conversations or reflections about diversity, wanting to protect their children from those issues as much as possible. Often, this kind of attitude gives children a binary worldview. However, that is why Caldwell's approach to diversity based on the Bible must be practiced in Korean immigrant churches and families. Therefore, I envision that dialogue on diversity, as Caldwell suggests, starts within sok gatherings and spreads to other groups. In this sense, sok gatherings can serve as microsystem scaffoldings for children's development and as experimental places to try to engage in various dialogues on diversity. Ensuring that soks are safe spaces and can include people with different needs is a role and responsibility of churches.

In this chapter, I have explored my theological emphasis on childhood and the shared responsibility of nurturing children in the faith community. I defined religious education for children as a communal effort and as a process of gathering meaningful building blocks to build a house of being in partnership with God. To build understanding of the world of emerging new second-generation Korean American children, I reviewed some of the cultural characteristics of Gen Z and Gen Alpha. They are the first generation of digital natives, conversant with rapidly developing technology and internet resources that connect them to the world in a second. They are also experiencing worldwide socioeconomic instability and violence from racial and religious conflicts. Thus, emerging new second-generation Korean American children are standing at the intersection of all these sociocultural, racial, religious, and technological dimensions. In this vein, I examined the cultural conflicts and racial stereotypes that these children confront in their homes and society and discussed racial identity development for Asian Americans. After reviewing major theories of child development, I suggested the sok practice as a scaffolding and as a safe place for children's faith and identity formation.

Going back to the case of Alice, I cannot know exactly what stages she has gone through in her family and surroundings because of my limited observations of her. Yet, based on Vygotsky's understanding, she has a strong scaffolding from her parents and grandparents. Her family members often expressed their hopes and plans for Alice and her education in preschool. Based on those conversations, I think she was being pushed (and will be pushed) to expand her zone of proximal development. For her family, there was no consistent mentoring community that could offer them guidance in nurturing their kids or in living as Christians. Her parents joined the

Sunday Bible study group, yet there was no strong sok gathering for young families like Alice's in that church.

    I still don't know whether Alice's behavior was all right or somewhat problematic for her own future. I still wish I could tell her parents that Alice felt and learned some things about herself and her surroundings and collected some building blocks during her Sunday experiences. I still wish I could engage in more thorough observations of her and her family and offer some proper support. For now, I can only pray that Alice grows up as a healthy and integrated second-generation Korean American in a loving community that supports her development and ethnic identity, so she is able to survive her own "shipwrecks," or life crises.[36]

---

36. S. Parks, *Big Questions, Worthy Dreams*, 39.

Chapter 5

COME PLAY IN OUR MADANG

IN THE PREVIOUS CHAPTERS, I identified and discussed the internalized model minority complex among Korean immigrants and their children, the banking model of education and the lack of faith development for all ages, and the generation gap as major issues for contemporary Korean American immigrant churches. Along with these complex issues, I revealed that Korean immigrant churches are not doing well in overcoming the generational tensions between those in the first and second generations. That means Korean immigrant churches do not serve as constructive havens for immigrants' religious and social development nor for Shin Yi Se (emerging new second-generation) children. I draw implications for Korean churches from the work of Elizabeth Caldwell with other churches. Caldwell has found that "what is missing in such congregations is an ethos of a faithful learning community that empowers by its planning for faithful learning across the ages. Or in other words, making a home as a learning and growing community of Christians has been forgotten or abandoned. The church as a place of homemaking with a great room of people, using content and methods that integrate worship, education, mission, stewardship, and community is here never considered."[1] The concerns Caldwell identifies should direct congregations toward finding alternative ways to create faithful learning communities. Korean congregations need to transform their traditional education systems and liberate their members from racial stereotypes and obsession with social success, while reconciling the generations with each other and other people in society.

---

1. Caldwell, "Religious Instruction," 78.

CONCEPTUAL FRAMEWORK OF MADANG: TOWARD REDEMPTIVE COMMUNITY

As a primary concept in constructing a new paradigm of faith formation, I present the idea of interdependence. This concept is an important reminder of how all human beings and nature, not just immigrant communities, influence each other and live together. Professor of preaching HyeRan Kim-Cragg, in her book *Interdependence: A Postcolonial Feminist Practical Theology*, imagines what it means to learn and grow through mutual dialogue and interdependence, rather than a one-way, top-down approach. Kim-Cragg says, "One of the enterprises of practical theology is to teach trust. To teach trust is to teach to question. To question is to doubt without falling into despair."[2] For Korean immigrants who are not familiar with challenging authority, teaching them how to doubt and ask questions based on trust and care is a radical, yet necessary, idea. One model for doing this is Freire's problem-posing approach to education, which is a pedagogy of dialogue between a teacher and a student involving mutual trust that moves beyond a hierarchical relationship.[3] The teacher's task in such a dialogue is not to replicate authoritarianism and oppression but to help students develop mutual learning by joining with them in their reality and problems and helping them become aware of the nature of their reality and being-ness through critical thinking.[4]

In this regard, the community of faith I dream of is not a place to silence marginalized opinions or differences, but a place where people can communicate with open minds and work together toward the creative transformation of the world.[5] Such a vision is strengthened by Jack Seymour's concept of redemptive community. In his definition, people in a redemptive community look for signs of God's realm in the midst of human life. They invite strangers and the marginalized to their table. They also "pray for relief; challenge the principalities and powers that feed fear and callousness; and work for community."[6] In a redemptive community, individuals encounter each other and the world through cooperative work for mutual understanding. Therefore, educating for redemptive community

---

2. Kim-Cragg, *Interdependence*, loc. 674–79 of 5054.
3. Van Gorder, "Children of the Oppressors," 20.
4. Van Gorder, "Children of the Oppressors," 24.
5. Freire, *Pedagogy of the Oppressed*, 84.
6. Seymour, "Pay Attention," 14.

means helping people do these types of things and challenging them to engage in reconciliation and transformation.⁷

The essays in the book *Educating for Redemptive Community* explore the concept of redemptive community and how to embody it in various contexts. As Mary Elizabeth Moore notes in the foreword, this book does not provide a formula for becoming a redemptive community, but rather shows people how to navigate toward becoming God's realm in different contexts and how to find hope on the way.⁸ The book is based on the ministry of Jesus as a vision of redemptive community, and it shows us the attitudes and concrete actions we must take as disciples of Jesus in order to move beyond social boundaries to transform the world.

Yet, this concept of a redemptive community for healing, reconciliation, and hope cannot be fully translated into Korean. When *Teaching the Way of Jesus*, one of Seymour's recent books, was translated into Korean, his language of "a community of redemption," or "the redemptive community," was commonly translated as "a community of salvation."⁹ Just as the word *redemption* is used in the same way as *salvation* in general,¹⁰ any Korean who is new to the concept of redemptive community may think about it as a community of salvation, regardless of the content and direction of Seymour's definition. Considering the Korean evangelical Christian culture that prioritizes personal spiritual salvation over social transformation, this term, *community of salvation*, may actually strengthen the logic of the exclusivist belief that salvation is only possible through believing in Christ. This seems to be no different from the community of faith paradigm that emphasizes salvation and mission only in and through the church. Thus, it is challenging to translate *redemptive community* into Korean. The term can only be translated and understood with additional defining words, such as "구원과 회복의 공동체" (community of salvation and reconciliation), or "구원과 변혁의 공동체" (community of salvation and transformation). Defining

---

7. Seymour, "Pay Attention," 16.

8. Moore, "Foreword," xvii.

9. Seymour, *Teaching the Way of Jesus*, 14, 15, 164. On each of these pages, Seymour describes what it means to build and live in "a community of redemption," "a redeemed community," and "the redemptive community." In the Korean translation, all of these appear to be the same term, 구원의 공동체, which means "a community of salvation." See Seymour, 예수님이 직접 가르쳐준 교육학, 51, 53, 274.

10. Moore, "Foreword," vii. When you look up the word *redemption* in *Harper's Encyclopedia of Religious Education*, you are redirected to the word *salvation*. Cully and Cully, s.v. "Redemption."

redemption not just a problem that arises in the process of translation. I have often been asked questions by evangelicals regarding how God's redemption relates to social justice. For them, *redemption* means the forgiveness of sins and the salvation of souls, which can only be granted through faith in Jesus. Therefore, I argue that the word *redemption*, which has traditionally been used in a very limited sense, should be liberated. By adhering to the term *redemptive community*, I want to recognize and rescue the word *redemption* from its limited use in the Christian tradition and to reinterpret it through the lens of postcolonial feminist practical theology and progressive religious education.

The authors of the book *Educating for Redemptive Community* also expand the vision of redemption. Here, Moore's description of what it means to live in a redemptive community is noteworthy:

> In the Christian tradition, [*redemption*] usually refers to salvation from sin and evil and/or salvation to a better, more faithful and whole, way of life, whether for individuals or for whole communities. The authors of this book identify redemption in more than one way, but they recognize that much has been lost or has gone terribly awry in this world and that the world is in need of redemption—redemption from the horrors of injustice and violence, and redemption to righteousness, justice, and peace. Further, they are convinced that education can be a pathway of redemption; it can transform human lives, indeed all of God's creation, from destruction and death into life. It can be a pathway for honoring the dignity of every being in God's cosmos and cultivating the goodness and beauty in every living soul and in the whole of God's creation. Education is thus a means of grace.[11]

In the Korean American context, a Madang is a place to experience and declare the divine presence in a way that goes beyond the exclusive formula of redemption, that connects the church and society, and that works across all boundaries.[12] The definition and purpose of Madang stems from theologian Rosemary Radford Ruether's claim that "the mission of church is to renew and fulfill the original mandate of creation to become a world of peace and justice."[13] This divine vision is revealed to the world through people living lives of peace and striving for justice.[14] Beyond the insights

11. Moore, "Foreword," xii.
12. Ruether, "Christian Quest," 10.
13. Ruether, "Christian Quest," 10.
14. Ruether, "Christian Quest," 11.

gained from Ruether's concept of a feminist redemptive community, I insist that we need to overcome ageism and racism in our communities. We must respect and be blessed by life itself, and not be focused on people's biological ages or the social status that comes with age. We must respect and be blessed by existence itself, not by social hierarchies or by a theology of prosperity that teaches that social success is God's blessing. We must love each other as children of God without regard for skin color. Therefore, the redemptive community I imagine through my approach of Madang is a place where people experience reconciliation and liberation beyond all social labels; a place where children and their dignity and creativeness are honored; a place beyond the hierarchical system where children and adults practice companionship with God; and a place where people experience the mystery of God's presence through playful experience together, not through competition or debates. Madang is my vision of a redemptive community, one that connects with the people, culture, faith, and heritage of the Korean context. Based on these understandings, I urge individuals, or individual churches, or individual religious groups, to get out of their own comfort zones and to gather in a Madang.

THE MADANG APPROACH

Definition and Goals

As I shared briefly in chapter 1, the Korean word *madang* refers to the front courtyard (*ahp-madang*) or the backyard (*duit-madang*) of traditional Korean houses. It also refers to the courtyard of a community building or private house. For example, the courtyard of a church can be called the madang. This is not a publicly open space like a square or a plaza, but it is a space that people in the congregation can freely access and where they can talk with others.

Traditional Korean houses generally have fences or walls surrounding them. Before entering a house, which is the private space of a family, one first enters through the front gate and crosses the courtyard. This courtyard, the madang, is a space where the homeowner and guests greet each other and engage in various activities. For instance, in the madang, the host family might invite relatives and neighbors to join them in a meal, a birthday party, a wedding ceremony, or a funeral service. The madang in a house is, therefore, a private and a public space at the same time. Here, people communicate with their neighbors and share the joys and sorrows of life.[15] Here, people in a higher social class welcome people in a lower class to an event. In this space, conversations and activities take place with no regard for age, gender, or class. In other words, the madang is a place of reciprocal communication and communal interaction between people dealing with both happy and sorrowful moments and who have both similarities and differences.

Today in South Korea, at least in a metropolitan area like Seoul, it is not easy to find traditional houses with a madang, as these spaces have been replaced by apartment complexes. However, the concept of the madang has not completely disappeared; now virtual spaces are referred to as madangs, or the term is used conceptually when talking about inviting and embracing others. In other words, the madang is a virtual reality, such as a public bulletin board of a web community, and it continues to be a space for gathering and conversation between people, regardless of social class or location.

Moreover, it is noteworthy that the madang has been a space for various activities, including playing, but not for studying information. In general, studying traditionally took place inside the house. The madang was a place where children did outside activities, while still staying on private property. Here I am paying attention to the concept of "play." Unlike adults who work productively and systematically for a living, children engage in "play."[16] According to Kim-Cragg, "This work-play binary belittles the role of play as unproductive, the thing to be grown out of once children reach adulthood."[17] We should not underestimate what the seemingly immature and unstructured activities of children can bring to light. Feminist practical theologian Bonnie Miller-McLemore also makes this point, saying, "Play deeply shapes the texture of our daily life. In the best moments, it opens up space for encounter with God. Figuring out just how and why family play is so important to the life of faith is my task now, a task made more important by the challenges families face."[18] With this understanding, using the educational approach of play is a way to create a more equitable and mutual learning space in Korean-American immigrant churches, beyond the hierarchical tensions of adult-child, teacher-student, and parent-child

15. D. K. Lee, "마당, 아직 잃어버리지 않았다."

16. Kim-Cragg, *Interdependence*, loc. 470 of 5054. See also Hyun, *Making Sense of DCAP*, 15–30.

17 Kim-Cragg, *Interdependence*, loc. 475–76 of 5054.

18. Miller-McLemore, *In the Midst of Chaos*, 128.

relationships. This educational approach, with its less structured interactions, can be a fundamental and efficient method for breaking down high fences between individuals.

In chapter 4, I examined the developmental and cultural characteristics of growing second-generation children and identified the small group as one element that can help them grow in healthy ways and form their identities. A sok is a small group unit that helps each child and family member gather their own meaning blocks and build a sturdy house. The church is where such soks can be encouraged and organically connected. A Madang, then, is a liberating playground that helps each person and group in the church dialogue with others and the world (figure 9).

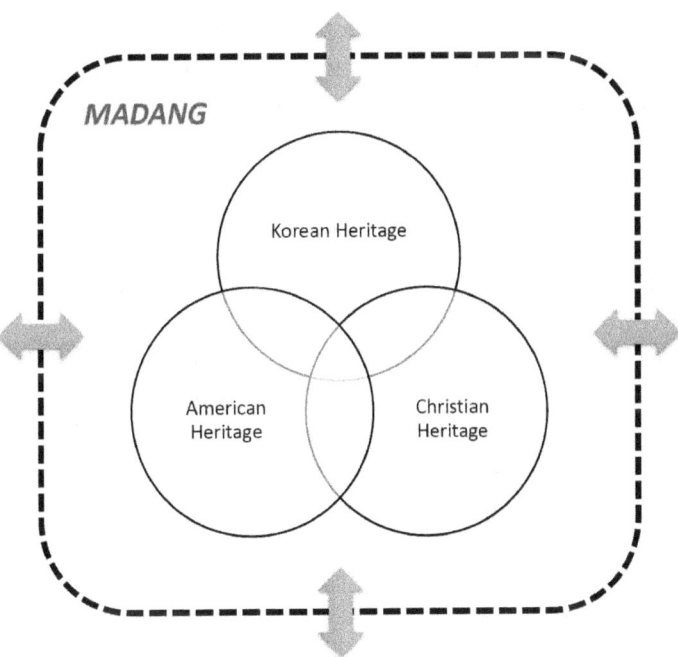

Figure 9. Madang as a liberating playground for a house of being

The Madang approach is a new way for Shin Yi Se, or emerging new second-generation Korean American children, to be creative and to be free from both internal and external conflicts that come from living in between two (or more) worlds. It is also a way to trigger more diverse cultural discourses.[19] Caldwell, emphasizing the experiential learning process, argues that "we know and practice the value of experiential learning with children and youth, yet we often fail to value these learning processes with adults."[20] The methods of the Madang approach are based on experiencing and playing, rather than on the traditional educational methods of knowledge transfer and memorization.[21] Children's play has a profound impact on their development and learning. Through play they learn social relations, roles, and values.[22] Play is now a methodology that adults need to learn again and participate in together with children.[23]

The power of play urges us religious educators to make a paradigm shift in the existing teaching-learning system. I consider play to be the most effective element for breaking down the oppressive system created by existing theological, educational, and cultural elements. Therefore, it is urgent that we guide Korean American children out of the current oppressive cultural and religious educational structure, help them unlearn the depositing model of education, and guide them to relearn the possibility of mutual transformation in church and society.

In her book *The Grace of Playing: Pedagogies for Leaning into God's New Creation*, practical theologian Courtney Goto examines Jürgen Moltmann's theology of play and introduces his ecclesiology: "I also find it helpful that Moltmann identifies the church as a key place for the kind of liberative playing he describes. He calls the church to be a 'testing ground' of the kingdom of God. . . . He identifies churches as vital places where playing is taking place and where he hopes Christians will experience faith more often. Moltmann encourages me to take seriously the role of churches in facilitating playing."[24] I resonate with Moltmann's and Goto's understanding of the church as a place to practice the kin-dom of God. In a Madang, first- and second-generation Korean Americans, adults and children, Christians and people of other religions, and straight and LGBTQIA+ people can finally come together and coexist. The goal is to experience the love of God and others beyond age, religion, language, sex, sexual orientation, or gender identity.

19. Goto, "Asian American Practical Theologies," loc. 1070–75 of 8057.
20. Caldwell, "Religious Instruction," 85.
21. Kim-Cragg, *Interdependence*, loc. 484–88 of 5054.
22. Hyun, *Making Sense of DCAP*, 15.
23. Hamman, "Playing," 42.
24. Goto, *Grace of Playing*, 47.

Principles and Steps

The educational approach of Madang is a process of living out one's own theology and the gospel by practicing the love of God and reconciling with others.[25] The experience of playing with others in a Madang engages individuals in healthy faith and identity development and social transformation. Individuals who have grown up with a good self-esteem and self-respect in a healthy community of faith are able to seek reconciliation and justice beyond religion and race.[26] Jack Seymour, in his book *Teaching the Way of Jesus*, explores the historical, theological, and educational aspects of what it means to live as a follower of Jesus. He suggests that we followers of Jesus have a responsibility to critically reflect on history and theologies, cooperate with other religious communities, and socially transform the future.[27] If we do not believe in such possibilities, there is no way to answer the challenges that Shin Yi Se children bring to the table. They are already encountering various social changes and the challenges of anti-Asian racism, the constant messages of various media, and reconciling church teachings with interactions with LGBTQIA+ students at school. If the Korean immigrant church insists on practicing an exclusive faith and ignoring the world, there is no future for it. There is no hope. But we can coexist with others and other religions based on our Christian faith and diverse cultural heritages through the understanding and practice of redemptive community. I insist that the task of religious educators is to guide people to see God's vision of the redemptive community and to present concrete and practical ways for them to build upon the creative possibilities within them.[28] In that regard, here I offer three principles of the Madang approach as a creative learning space for all people in order to lay a foundation for redemptive community in Korean immigrant congregations.

1. *Mutuality.* This communal space is based on relationships. It is important to acknowledge and respect one's conversation partners. Only with mutually influential beings can Madang be meaningfully established. If there is only you, an individual, or one religious body, Madang cannot exist. Madang is therefore based on mutual invitation, respect, and interdependence.

---

25. Kim-Cragg, *Interdependence*, loc. 3732–33.
26. Seymour, *Teaching the Way of Jesus*, 181.
27. Seymour, *Teaching the Way of Jesus*, 181–82.
28. Seymour, "Pay Attention," 20, 24.

2. *Understanding and Compromise.* A Madang is not a place for discussions that arrive at one correct answer; rather, it is a place of interaction in which people reveal various aspects of their lives to each other in order to enhance mutual understanding and to reflect on their own interpretations. It is a place of compromise rather than confrontation. Rather than being a place for making one's own arguments or prescriptions, it is a place for practicing an attitude of listening to others.

3. *Movement.* The purpose of all dialogue is to move toward common action. Whether one is gathering for a pre-determined act or setting up an action plan for a common good based on the results of a conversation, the purpose of a Madang is to learn and to fulfill God's loving will for the world, which is social justice through solidarity. Opening the doors of churches and temples for interreligious dialogue and designing programs for believers in other traditions are good examples of the activism of Madang. Leading a campaign against global climate change or offering trauma counseling opportunities to hate crime survivors can also be good movements.

I argue that the Madang approach is a Christian educational method that is not only generated from Koreans and the Korean diaspora's cultures, but it also reflects the practices of other cultures and the spirit of the early Christian communities. I am confident that it is an approach worth trying by all Christians and by all generations who dream of their faith communities being transformed and moving beyond their current religious and social boundaries.[29] Based on such a vision and the principles I have listed, the Madang approach is comprised of four steps.

1. *Entering*: sharing daily life or major events

    Madang presupposes mutual respect and understanding. The equitable and neutral space of a Madang is also a holy space where mutual dependence, recovery, and transformation are possible when participants share their struggles, hopes, and dreams. The leader of a Madang welcomes the participants and begins the meeting with a greeting of peace and prayer. Participants are encouraged to share their life events.

2. *Exploring*: reading texts within their biblical and historical contexts

---

29. Wimberly, *Soul Stories*, 1.

In the Madang, participants will read and examine biblical texts in depth. The leader or a designated person can share the historical context and any background information about the texts for deeper engagement.

3. *Playing*: reading the texts through the lenses of daily life and applying them to real cases

   Next, it is time to play in the Madang according to the given rules, which are the texts of the day, and to share interpretations of the texts. Adults can mainly utilize discussion as a form of a play. They can reflect on the texts and share how they can manifest meaning and God's aims in their daily lives or social events. For children, Madang is a time for conversation, application, and activities. The purpose is to go beyond an instructional model of education and to allow children to freely imagine, share their lives, and share ideas that can be applied to their respective situations. This is not a time to brag or to compete over who knows more. It should be a time to remind children of each other's unique value in God's eyes.

4. *Blessing*: imagining a concrete action plan for families, neighbors, and society

   This is the stage for thinking about how God's people can serve and bless the world.[30] The leader encourages the people who have gathered in the Madang to share their lives and faith and guides them to see how they can collectively work for social change. As participants discern the divine presence and their vocations, they are invited to make commitments and develop concrete action plans.[31]

In our multiracial and multiethnic society, God's hospitality is a vital attitude that we should practice as Christians. Sarah Shin says, "The solution is not to be colorblind. The solution is to start by building trust. Ethnicity-aware trust-building is essential to inviting people to Jesus' table. We must offer the hospitality of God to a racially and ethnically broken world by adopting and embodying cross-cultural skills."[32] In the Madang

---

30. This is one of my favorite images of the church community: "Now we understand that it is the people of God who gather for worship, learning, fellowship, and service. But the church is also all of us when we scatter for our larger vocations in the world." Crain, *United Methodist Deacon*, 11.

31. Wimberly, *Soul Stories*, 34; Seymour, *Teaching Biblical Faith*, 55.

32. Shin, *Beyond Colorblind*, 103.

educational space, rather than being hostile to or exclusionary with each other, people will actively invite others and talk openly for mutual understanding and transformation. Thus, the Korean immigrant church will not simply be an ethnic shelter away from the mainstream society, but rather a cross-cultural incubator that fosters open and creative dialogues with others. The process of coming out of oppressive structures and participating in play more freely and creatively is a process of relearning God's redemptive love and grace for all.

The Madang approach is about opening ourselves to other people and moving beyond existing practices of cultural exclusiveness by inviting others into our lives and accepting their invitations. Here, I see the possibility of redemptive community and the role of religious education. The purpose of the church community and religious education is to help people find the meanings of their lives and follow divine callings. Personal trauma or relational struggles should be healed and overcome. The Madang space is not intended to hurt or oppress anyone. What we need to unlearn is the oppressive religious interpretations and practices of the church. What we need to relearn is love and mutual transformation. In Korean American churches, there are those who experience healing in faith and relationships. There are people who dream and work hard to change their communities for their children. As long as there are such people, there is hope, and there is community. Then the responsibility of scholars and religious educators like me is to develop approaches, cast new visions, and embody them.

As one practices the Madang approach, the key questions one needs to ask are as follows: (1) Is this type of educational process mutually respectful, recognizing different people's spaces and struggles? (2) Does it lead to an open discussion, where people seek answers together and learn from each other? and (3) Does it lead to concrete action plans that can be implemented? With these questions in mind, one may want to see an example of what the Madang educational approach might look like in a congregational setting.

AN EXAMPLE OF THE MADANG APPROACH

During the years 2020 and 2021, I collaborated with Korean American pastors and scholars to develop a Bible study guide for Korean immigrant churches called 함께 이루어가는 하나님 나라 [*The Kin-dom of God We Build*

Together].³³ The project was a meaningful one since it dealt with the reality of our lives as well as biblical interpretation, especially in terms of being immigrants living in the United States. I hope this Bible study guide will continue to be a resource to congregations for discussing various issues in society and interpreting them faithfully, as well as an inspiration for developing additional study guides for different groups of people in the future.

The Kin-dom of God We Build Together was written for young adults and adults, but a few chapters are suitable for all ages. For example, lesson 2, "A Fruitful and Prosperous Life," discusses environmental issues and climate change based on Genesis 1:1—2:4. It points out that climate change is one of the major causes of the spread of the coronavirus. Environmental justice is emphasized as a means to restore the relationship between humans and God as well as with creation. Lesson 4, "War and Unification: The Road to Reconciliation and Peace," examines the history of the division of Korea and presents theological insights through the reconciliation process that occurred between Jacob and Esau in Genesis 33. Based on Genesis 1:26–27 and Acts 10:23–38, Lesson 7 discusses having an anti-racist Christian attitude and the responsibility to be an anti-racist. Lesson 8, which I wrote, was about the Christian task of creating gender equality, and as a biblical example, I dealt with the cooperative ministry of Priscilla and Aquila (Acts 18, Romans 16:3–4). For further discussion, three newspaper articles related to gender discrimination at home, at work, and at church were presented as examples.

Each lesson was developed following common guidelines, and the specific steps are as follows:

1. Introduction
2. Opening Reflection: Context—What's Going On?
3. Scripture Reading: Text—What's the Bible Saying?
4. Close Look: Studying the Text and Context
5. Theological Interpretation
6. Application to Life
7. Closing Prayer

A separate manual for the leader was also published, which included questions for discussion. A closing prayer, scriptures for daily meditation,

---

33. UMC Peace Initiative, 함께 이루어가는 하나님 나라.

and a recommended reading list were included at the end of each lesson. The study guide incorporates the three principles that I presented earlier: mutuality, understanding and compromise, and movement, as well as the four steps of the Madang approach: entering, exploring, playing, and blessing. Through collaboration with other pastors and theologians, my vision of Madang education came alive. It was an opportunity to see how this work might expand and develop in the future. The possibilities of the Madang approach are not only found in this curriculum. I have already witnessed various examples of Madang practices and their potential. In the next chapter, I will discuss these seeds of my hope.

Chapter 6

SIGNS OF MADANG, THE REDEMPTIVE COMMUNITY

THE MADANG APPROACH IS not an entirely new idea I came up with. The foundation for this educational method can be found in the biblical tradition and early Christian communities. The Korean culture, which values community activities, reinforces this practice and guides us to imagine the Madang space. The roots of the Madang practice can also be found in the Wesleyan small group movement. Madang education is actually happening everywhere! You can find hints for application and a yearning for an alternative educational method in various research studies and congregational practices.

I agree with Goto when she points to playing together as a way of participating in the full experiences of joy and sorrow and of being able to build new hope in God's realm.[1] It is the duty of religious educators, therefore, to ensure that church communities can lead the process of playing together and moving toward the new creation of God. For such a creative process, Goto presents some practical approaches that churches can use to apply play in their ministries: "For a visual arts church, this might mean teaching people to see connections between images and theology. For a musical church, this might entail teaching the faithful a deeper appreciation for music and theology, for a foodie church, food and theology. This kind of teaching and learning might involve experiential learning, critical reflection, and discussion. In addition, it would hopefully assist learners to perceive God's beauty more fully in experiences appropriate to their LPTA [local practical theological aesthetics]."[2]

1. Goto, *Grace of Playing*, 53. See also Hamman, "Playing," 49.
2. Goto, *Grace of Playing*, 112.

These examples are also applicable to the Madang approach. The Madang approach can lead children to play using visual or musical elements. For example, using a variety of colors, leaders can encourage multicultural/multiethnic children to learn about each other's differences and dignity and then reflect on and discuss what God's hospitality looks like. Kathryn Otoshi's picture book *One* can be a good conversation starter for this process. Simply with round splashes of watercolors, Otoshi explores different personalities, the issue of bullying, and the practice of reconciliation. By reading the picture book together and following that with an activity and conversation, both children and adults can grasp the idea of respecting different people.

Goto's idea of linking food with theology can be applied to Korean immigrant church education. Especially because food is one of the important parts of sok gatherings, such gatherings can be a great opportunity for Shin Yi Se children to learn about Korean culture and food. Children and adults can also discuss foods, bodies, and theology, like how God cared for people in the Bible by providing food. Here again, a children's book can be used as a conversation starter. Linda Sue Park's *Bee-Bim Bop!* introduces the meaning of and recipe for one of the most popular traditional Korean dishes. Since it is a picture book in English about a Korean dish, it can be a good resource not only for immigrant parents and their young children, but also for churches and organizations preparing for community events. Becoming familiar with a traditional Korean dish and sharing personal histories or memories of it can be a part of Madang play. By making the dish together, children will integrate this food play into their own experience. While traditional Korean Christian education does not consider making food or communicating about friendship a part of teaching, the Madang approach encourages learning to take place through such experiential play with one another.

Moreover, the work of Madang is valid in the era of the COVID-19 pandemic and the post-pandemic era. For children who feel comfortable and at ease meeting and chatting online, the Madang community can expand globally through virtual spaces. In her recent publication, *Invisible: Theology and the Experience of Asian American Women*, Grace Ji-Sun Kim points out that Korean women traditionally had to stay in private spaces, separated and isolated from social and masculine spaces, and that the madang was a place for women's activities.[3] Then Kim launched a podcast

---

3. G. J. Kim, *Invisible*, 27.

project called *Madang*, which demonstrates the possibility of creatively expanding this space of interaction. For her podcasts, Kim invites other scholars from different social locations and disciplines and engages them in various discussions. She begins each podcast by saying, "Madang is the outdoor living room of the world. Here, we invite you to sit and tune into unreserved, remarkable conversations with renowned authors, leaders, public figures and scholars on religion, culture and everything in-between."[4] Kim's podcast is a great resource for scholarly discussions on current issues and theology, and a great example of the use of the virtual Madang.

Again, the Madang approach is not only theoretical but also practical. The findings from my ethnographic research reveal the potential of Madang education. Despite the multilayered problems that Korean immigrant churches have been experiencing, they have not given up. Struggling to find breakthroughs on their own, they have been trying to find new ways of being the church by taking one small step at a time. As I suggested in previous chapters, Korean immigrant churches' sok meetings can be base camps in which Shin Yi Se children can experience life-giving community. I witnessed the possibility of such a sok meeting in an interview with Alice.

SOK PRACTICE FOR THE SHIN YI SE

Alice, a 1.5-generation Korean American, had been attending an English service at a Korean church in her neighborhood. Since joining Hope Church three years ago, her family had become comfortable attending a small English service at Hope Church, in which thirty youth and young adults worshiped together. The only English-speaking sok among the ten soks at the church had especially become a harbor for Alice's family. Alice shared,

> But it's rather good. It's more like a friend, in solidarity. My sok is like a family. We've been together for over a year now. It's the second year now. It's like a family. It's like a family. I can share everything with them . . . I mean, people are so good in my sok. It hasn't been that long, but they treat me like a family or a friend. I mean, we now have a mentor that we never had before. Mr. Choi and his family . . . My husband and I wish to be like Mr. and Mrs. Choi after ten or twenty years. I cannot hope for anything better. I haven't had such an example before. I have met so many Christians, but

---

4. G. J. Kim, *Madang*.

> I haven't seen such selfless, devoted people, except a pastor or a pastor's wife. We felt that. So, we decided to learn from them.

Many Koreans seem to prefer a diversity of activities and relationships, or anonymity, based on the attendance at the mega-sized Korean immigrant churches in the metropolitan area where Hope Church is also located. However, encouragingly, people were still gathering at and visiting this relatively small congregation, seeking a community of people who can live together like an extended family based on intimate relationships with and mentorship of one another. There is also the presence of passionate and devoted leaders for younger generations, people whom Alice considers to be mentors.[5] Based on such an example of nurturing, Alice herself committed to becoming a mentor for a younger generation:

> Alice: Yes. There are not many young adults. Only three female young adults. Because they said they need a mentor, because they are now just 23 or 24 years old. They need someone so desperately. Because their mothers and fathers are too old, and the pastor of the English service is a young male. They needed a female mentor. They needed someone who understands living in America as a woman and a Christian. Then, there is only me for them, now, in this situation. So I said okay, let's do it. Let's read a book together . . .
>
> Me: Oh, that's so nice.
>
> Alice: Yes. They really need that kind of supporting presence. Because I also thought it would have been very helpful if I could have had someone like that at that age. But I didn't have.

In terms of sociocultural generations, Alice and her spouse are part of Gen X, which is now the most active age group in churches and society. According to the history of Korean immigration, Alice's and her spouse's timeline corresponds to the third wave of immigration.[6] Based on Asian American studies, they can be recognized as part of the new second generation.[7] Alice is part of a hybrid new second generation that came to the United States with her family as immigrants in the mid-1980s, and she is fortunate to be able to participate in either English-speaking or Korean-speaking congregations without difficulty. This generation could also be referred to as the lost generation, the generation of Koreans who couldn't

---

5. Chung, "Mozying," 58.
6. J. H. Kim, *Bridge-Makers and Cross-Bearers*, 6.
7. Jeung, Chen, and Park, "Identities of the New Second Generation," 4–5.

effectively adapt to American culture in between the poles of being Korean and American.[8] How many times have we Koreans seen the phenomenon of second-generation Koreans leaving the church after graduating from high school? I recall Jeremiah and the people of Israel, who cried helplessly while watching the city of Jerusalem fall apart. I recall the tears of parents crying out for help for their children departing from their homes and churches. With these examples in mind, I have lamented the decline of the church.

Nonetheless, Alice is an example of an active, hybrid new second-generation person who copes and adapts to the different cultures she lives in and tries to heal herself and heal others in a shelter-like or family-like community. I witnessed a seed of hope in Alice's hoping to become the type of Christian her mentors are by mentoring younger Korean Americans through her time and affection. Of course, there is still much to do. The loss of young people continues to be a serious phenomenon throughout mainstream churches as well as Korean churches, as young people are still leaving their churches after high school. However, I have seen Alice's community experience and mentoring experience—showing there is no completely lost generation—and thus a new shoot has sprouted from the ashes of my former despair. This is the beginning of the redemptive community. It is a community where the oppressed do not stand as oppressors, but overturn the experience of suffering and spread the message of love and salvation like a wild wind.

VARIOUS BONDING OPPORTUNITIES

In order to expand redemptive community experiences, my interviewees shared that they would like to have more bonding opportunities for adults as well as children. Parents want more concrete and theological conversation opportunities about faith, life, and parenting. They also want children to have more activities on weekdays in addition to worship and Bible study on Sundays. This shows why Madang education is necessary and how it should be applied. We need to remember once again that education ministry volunteers are repeating the banking model of education because they have not experienced any other alternatives. In that sense, the suggestions I have given for better congregational education are important elements for developing various Madang approaches in the future. While Madang

---

8. Kang, "Reflections Upon Methodology," 409. See also J. Y. Lee, *Marginality*, 45.

education can take many forms, I am going to share three methods for working toward this type of redemptive community: (1) kids' discipleship classes and retreats, (2) parents' prayer meetings, and (3) mission outreach experiences.

Kids' Discipleship Classes and Retreats

Among their churches' children's programs, every interviewee positively evaluated the fourth- and fifth-grade discipleship classes, which are prototypes of children's sok meetings. The discipleship classes are a program that has been going on for decades in the children's ministries of Hope Church and Future Church. The classes have been held in the churches or in members' homes for six to eight weeks in the spring and fall, for two to three hours each weekend. The classes have been conducted by the children's pastor or director. During each session, the children communicate with each other in a relaxed and comfortable environment, share food, and engage in activities related to Bible study. At the end of the program, children participate in service activities in the area with the adult mission team or have a field trip. For many children, this becomes their first encounter with local needs—by handing out bags of sandwiches to homeless people, for example. As you see in this example, this program fits well with the Madang approach's four steps: entering, exploring, playing, and blessing.

Here is another example of Madang education: In an upper elementary Friday Bible class at Hope church, the class started by eating a dinner that one of the parents had prepared for the occasion, and the participants spent half of the time chatting with each other. After the table gathering, the teacher reviewed the lessons they had learned the previous week and then continued with a lesson related to the Bible, which was accompanied by crafts and games. The six children who participated seemed to be comfortable with the setting and participated in the activities happily. The teacher reported, "When they went up to grade six, the result [of the discipleship class during fifth grade] was amazingly good. [The class] was necessary. The kids were so well adapted [with each other and the youth ministry]. They were prepared well for that transition. Something made them ready. Well, then, even if it is difficult [to commit my time every weekend], we should continue."

In a time when the purposes and influences of church education are losing their light, I witnessed this small group of people trying to live out a divine calling. Given the various circumstances of modern society and culture, it is difficult to encourage any volunteers to dedicate each weekend to educating children. Nevertheless, parents and volunteers who share the importance of this time in children's lives continue to gather and work to make their education programs better.

In addition, Future Church and Hope Church (occasionally with other English-speaking Korean American congregations in the area) offer an annual retreat for fourth and fifth graders. For two nights and three days, children have worship and fellowship experiences at a retreat center. This event marks the completion of their weekly discipleship program and helps them transition to youth ministries. It is also one of the core programs of the churches' children's ministries and encourages lower elementary children and their families to expect such experiences in the future. For the success of the retreat, coordination with parents is absolutely necessary. As long as the conditions and restrictions of the retreat center permit it, many parent volunteers join together to make Korean foods and snacks for the two nights and three days. Traditionally, spicy ramen cups, which are not eaten at school, have been a favorite snack at the retreat. At one retreat, there were some children who came to the volunteers to make sure there would be enough spicy ramen cups for everyone to eat after having s'mores at the campfire.

These activities not only provide children with bonding opportunities, but also are alternatives that overcome the limitations of the banking model of education in Korean immigrant churches. Ultimately, it turned out that parents do not actually expect the banking model of Bible study for their children. As Alice pointed out, education ministries need to offer more opportunities to discuss what it means to live as Christians in this world and to use various Christian education approaches that provide not only religious instruction, but also opportunities for spiritual growth, faith community development, social transformation, and interfaith dialogue.[9]

Parents' Prayer Meetings

No matter how tough or lonely their lives get, all immigrant parents want the best for their children. These parents' wishes are not just for their children—they also aspire to have their own communities in which people care for one another. All of my interviewees revealed their longing for

---

9. Seymour, "Approaches to Christian Education," 21.

community and a thirst for their own peer experiences. Many respondents told me that they would like to have a place where they can meet, converse, pray, and talk about parenting on a weekly basis. Hyejin said,

> Because you only go to church once a week, you must have faith education at home. My sister confessed that her daughter left her church when she went to college, saying that she didn't do much faith education at home. To be honest, there is a church I want to join in my neighborhood. There are a lot of school friends of my son there, and a great parents' prayer meeting in the youth ministry. The good thing about the youth pastor there is that once a week he calls parents and updates them about activities and prayer requests, and parents gather on weekdays to talk and pray together. That's what parents do. That's what parent education should be. That's important. How important is that!

Hyejin compared the youth pastors and ministries of the Korean churches in her neighborhood and expressed the importance of the continuing dedication of the staff and an organized gathering of parents throughout the week. Of course, it is true that the success-driven faith and education model can be reinforced in these parent meetings. It is also true, however, that such meetings can be a key chance for parent education that engages parents in constructive conversations that are beneficial to them and their children.

Eunju commented on what she had heard from other mothers and lamented the lack of such assistance from her church:

> You know what the kids are going through at school, through conversations. I know from the unnies ["older sisters," i.e., older mothers in the neighborhood] around me, they tell me what to expect when my children go to youth group . . . But you only get the abstract or irrelevant stories from the church. There is nothing wrong with such stories, but there is no concrete way to cope with real issues. As a parent, I would like to learn more specifically how to talk with my children about faith and life.

In the same vein, Alice said,

> The commitment of teachers is very important. I've been thinking about it for a while. I think our pastors and teachers are doing their best. And the teachers are trying to do their own hard work, but there is something missing. On the other hand, parents also should be deeply involved [in children's faith education], but there

are not many parents' meetings in Sunday school. I think if you just send your child to Sunday school, you have to be interested in it and help out. If there is something you can contribute, you have to work together for a child. I hope [the education ministry] will provide the necessary resources and training for specific care and nurture for individuals.

These are recurrent stories from many parents and teachers. After all, parents of young children want to talk more specifically about social and cultural issues while having their children's education based on Christian beliefs. Inevitably, Korean immigrant parents have a high dependence on and high expectations for their churches. However, responses and changes in Korean immigrant church education are slower in coming than social changes. It is urgent that churches offer Madang educational opportunities and proactively communicate with parents and educate them so that gaps between daily life and faith can be narrowed.

Mission Outreach Experiences: Living Out Faith

One of the principles and key steps of the Madang approach is blessing: making commitments to social justice. This focus can be easily forgotten in the typical Bible study, where students study Bible facts and the relevancy of the gospel to current social issues is dismissed or omitted. Yet, there is still a possibility of bringing up a focus on serving neighbors and working to dismantle systemic injustices up front. I found clues for doing this in some congregational outreach programs.

My interviewee Kay stated that the most positive aspects of Future Church's education ministry are the children's retreat and the mission outreach experiences. Their son went through the children's ministry program at Future Church and is currently attending the youth service, and their younger son is in the children's ministry. Kay stated,

> It is also very important that there is a church that we can trust and send our kids to. We participate in most of the church's programs, meaning that we don't do many other social activities. My bottom line is to let my kids participate in all the church events for them. The good thing is that my kids love to go to a retreat or on a week-long mission trip. I think it's important as a believer. It is important to have knowledge of the Bible while growing up, of course. But when I think of myself in the past, the things I realized while doing such mission service seem to be the most meaningful—about

life, the world, injustice, vocation, and so on, you know. I hope my children can have a community of service throughout their experiences now. It is not simple and easy to form such a community. Especially in this society, isn't it? I hope my kids realize the importance of service and action, along with Bible study or spiritual practice. It's beyond all of that.

Kay's story summarizes well what parents expect from faith education: they want Christian religious education to enable people from a young age to live and act beyond the knowing level of faith. In other words, churches should provide opportunities for service and encourage members to engage in social justice activities. Kay's testimony proves why we need the Madang approach, why it is critical to encourage people in the Madang to gather and then scatter to serve and bless the world. By providing sok practices and various bonding opportunities for children and their families, Korean American churches are sowing the seeds of transformation.

CONCLUSION

AT THE BEGINNING OF this book, I introduced Yolanda Smith's triple-heritage model of Christian education and translated her three heritages of African American Christians into three heritages of Korean American Christians. Then I suggested that meaningful relationships are the central piece at the intersection of these three heritages. Asian Canadian religious educator Greer Anne Wenh-In Ng, in her article "Family and Education from an Asian North-American Perspective: Implications for the Church's Educational Ministry," also discusses three distinctive cultural influences for Asian North American children: "(a) the heritage culture; (b) the dominant culture; and (c) the culture of the Christian faith community."[1] She emphasizes that, unlike mainstream groups, which generally deal with only two cultures—religious and social—ethnic minority groups need to create a balance in faith education between three cultures.[2] Thus, for Korean Americans, religious interpretation and teaching should not be focused on solidifying social systems based on the logic of mainstream society, nor should educators mislead their congregations with so-called "irrelevant Biblical teachings" unrelated to the social and political positions of Korean Americans.[3] In addition, Korean immigrant churches should not overlook the characteristics of our global society in the twenty-first century and the realities of the younger generations in their teachings and religious practices.

As one way to reach out and nurture people of younger generations, I have examined the sok practices of Korean immigrant churches. The sok

1. Ng, "Family and Education," 57.
2. Ng, "Family and Education," 57.
3. Shin, *Beyond Colorblind*, 7.

is a communal approach that can empower children and their families to develop their faith and racial identities together. The possibility of a sok serving as an extended family is supported by Alice's statements found in chapter 6. Alice found a trustworthy and dependable group of people and a mentor through a sok, and as a result, she was becoming a mentor for some young adults in her congregation. However, having such a structure does not guarantee that the faith education that takes place in it is theologically sound. Therefore, what is necessary is to shift the paradigm to provide sound theological educational guidelines, so that, whatever format a church has, faith education can lead to a transformation of people's minds "toward more life-giving possibilities, draw from the riches of their creative stories, and show promising pathways that can lead the way."[4] As Paulo Freire and Henry Giroux, prominent scholars of critical pedagogy, claim, education is not simply about teaching skills or methods.

The primary task of education is to help students critically understand and judge the social and structural problems of society and the power relations that create them.[5] In that sense, if the church does not help its members reflect critically about their faiths and their lives in general and help them engage proactively in social conversations and take actions for justice, churches' educational and communal structures will be merely empty shells.[6] According to Joel Spring, a scholar of educational policies, "Students are empowered when they gain the knowledge and critical understanding required to improve the social and economic conditions of the world. At the heart of empowerment is the search for methods of eliminating social injustice and decreasing inequalities in power."[7] Therefore, educational guidelines that encourage critical thinking and dialogue in healthy theology should be provided within Korean immigrant church communities so they don't become "institutional breeding grounds for commercialism, racism, social intolerance, sexism, and homophobia."[8]

As I discussed in chapter 2, being like a child means recognizing our interdependence with God and others. Beyond any social successes, we need to remember the preciousness of life itself and the value of weaving relationships of total trust and interdependence with God and the world.

---

4. Goto, "Asian American Practical Theologies," loc. 1072–73.
5. Giroux, *On Critical Pedagogy*, 71, 155; Spring, *Wheels in the Head*, 27.
6. Giroux, *On Critical Pedagogy*, 81.
7. Spring, *Wheels in the Head*, 27. See also Giroux, "Rethinking Education," 715–21.
8. Giroux, *On Critical Pedagogy*, 83.

The community that values human beings' ontological identity as children of God becomes a redemptive, life-giving community. In this community, the children of God invite us into their Madang. They want to go beyond the logic of human power and to play and experience life together in God's grace and love.

One of the main characteristics of Gen Z and Gen Alpha and their lives in a globalizing society is that they are always connected to the internet. OECD's current trend analysis emphasizes that "technologies not only connect people but also shape individual behaviors and abilities."[9] With the rapid development of technology, young people live in a local area and at the same time have connections around the world. They might be a member of a minority group in one place, but part of a mainstream culture elsewhere. They can find information they want by themselves, upload their own findings to social media, and enjoy the sense of sharing and belonging within the world. This means they are independent learners and teachers at the same time. For these young people, it may not make much sense to adapt to the mainstream culture and live within the constraints of only one or two identities. Looking at current technological developments and cultural trends, this will gradually become more evident.

I have argued that Madang can be a space for communication in the virtual world and a way to reach out to younger generations. Beyond a local church, which is physically located in one area and takes care of the religious life of a local congregation, the virtual Madang is a possible place for younger generations to gather and play with people around the world and to have theological and critical conversations as they encounter various cultural and social problems in their real and virtual spaces.

In Chapter 5, I presented three principles and four steps for implementing the Madang approach. This creative and liberating space presupposes mutuality, understanding and compromise, and movement. In this place, participants recognize each other for who they are, and they aim to learn from each other and grow together beyond the boundaries of age, race, sex, and gender identity. They also look for ways to connect cultural and social realities with faith and to transform their worlds in hope.[10] The practice of the Madang approach consists of four steps: entering, exploring, playing, and blessing. This approach allows students to participate in their religious education with their imaginations and to go beyond the

---

9. OECD, *Trends Shaping Education 2016*, 102.
10. Seymour, *Teaching Biblical Faith*, 64.

schooling-instructional paradigm.[11] The Madang approach is not an educational approach that depends on the qualities and abilities of a leader; rather, it aims for equality between all participants and the possibility of learning and growing with one another.

SUGGESTIONS FOR FUTURE WORK

I attempted to approach my study from various angles and to suggest new possibilities, despite the limited literature on Shin Yi Se, the emerging new second generation of Korean Americans. Still, there are many research topics to develop further.

My research started with an analysis of Gen Z and Gen Alpha. However, there are still not many resources that analyze these generations theologically or educationally. This was both exciting and frightening. I was concerned because not only was there no theological analysis of these young generations, there were only socio-economic approaches to them. In economics, these young generations are analyzed as potential consumers. Before they are treated and educated as the golden subjects of consumerism, they first should be approached as children of God. As Seymour insists, we religious educators need to present God's vision for them and offer concrete and practical ways to nurture them.

In this study, only the fundamental principles and some possible examples of the Madang approach were presented. Based on these, specific training materials for adults and children should be developed, for both Korean-speaking and English-speaking congregations. Jerome Berryman's series of books on his Godly Play methodology and Elizabeth Caldwell's "I wonder" approach for children are good examples of Madang-style education. So far, the only Bible study materials available for Korean American youth have been developed by evangelical religious educators. My challenge is to develop inclusive, progressive, and critical education programs using Madang principles.

During the ethnographic interviews I conducted, several parents asked if I could refer them to storybooks for young Korean American children. This request corresponds to what Wenh-In Ng says about the triple heritage. She insists that the three important cultures for immigrant children—"the Judaeo-Christian biblical tradition, the Euro-Anglo traditions of the dominant culture, and the traditions of their heritage culture"—must

---

11. Westerhoff, *Will Children Have Faith?*, 40–41.

be harmoniously developed.[12] Yet, there are not many resources that discuss how to combine religious education with ethnic cultures. This also connects to Sarah Shin's argument. Shin states, "If we do not know our ethnic story, the past, we are rootless. You cannot find a home for yourself if you don't know the home from which you came. And you will certainly be a poor guest in the house of others. A wise Asian American colleague said to me once, 'If we do not know who we are, we just end up taking from others.'"[13]

Therefore, in addition to teaching the Bible and its sociocultural applications, we should deliver well-told ethnic stories in churches. However, despite the interviewees being aware of what to do, they often told me that there were not many proper books to read with children. Many of the Bible picture books that young children enjoy are not in Korean, and many Korean stories for older children are not in English. There is a constant need to develop bilingual resources for cultural studies as well as Bible studies for Shin Yi Se children. Additionally, as Wenh-In Ng points out, "What is missing so far, however, are study guides with reflection and discussion questions, as well as with ideas for teacher-leaders on how to make biblical connections where appropriate, or on how to integrate certain cultural stories into existing church school/religious educational materials."[14] This is work a Madang curriculum must address.

Not only are educational materials needed, but parents must experience the Madang approach first in order to dismantle the old way of learning as well as to learn how to effectively educate their children. Various educational materials should be developed to provide unlearning opportunities for parents and volunteers who have already been taught in the traditional schooling-instructional way and to help children and volunteers develop the racial, cultural, and religious identities suitable for a new era.

INVITATION

In this book, I have examined theological understandings of childhood, the sociocultural characteristics of Shin Yi Se Asian Americans in a globalizing society, and theories of child development and faith development in order to point out the roles of Korean immigrant churches in young people's

12. Ng, "Beyond Bible Stories," 125.
13. Shin, *Beyond Colorblind*, 187.
14. Ng, "Beyond Bible Stories," 134.

lives and to describe an alternative educational approach for emerging new second-generation Korean American children and their families. Along with these foundational understandings, I revealed the concerns and hopes of first- and 1.5-generation Korean immigrant parents for their churches and for their children. Through ethnographic research in Korean American United Methodist congregations, I identified four categories of current issues in the lives and faiths of Korean immigrant churches: (1) community-oriented lifestyles; (2) aging congregations and the generation gap; (3) the banking model of education and a lack of faith formation opportunities for all ages, and (4) the internalized racial stereotype of the model minority.

As an alternative approach to religious education, I proposed the Madang approach as an application of redemptive community in the Korean Christian context. The Madang approach is designed to transform the success-driven mindset and the schooling-instructional model of education. The four steps of the Madang approach (entering, exploring, playing, and blessing) allow people to practice living in harmony across differences of age, race, gender, religion, and culture. All are welcome to God's Madang to experience divine love and grace. Our children are already there. They are waving their hands at you and inviting you to join in their play in this Madang. Will you join them?

BIBLIOGRAPHY

"2000–2009 Timeline Contents." *Future Timeline*. Accessed November 28, 2022. https://www.futuretimeline.net/21stcentury/2000-2009.htm.

"2010–2019 Timeline Contents." *Future Timeline*. Accessed November 28, 2022. https://www.futuretimeline.net/21stcentury/2010-2019.htm.

Aderoju, Darlene. "BTS Named Twitter's Most Popular Musical Act Again!—Marking 4 Consecutive Years for K-Pop Band." *People*, February 18, 2021. https://people.com/music/bts-named-twitter-most-popular-musical-act-for-fourth-consecutive-year/.

Alfonseca, Kiara. "There Have Been More Mass Shootings than Days in 2023, Database Shows." *ABCNews*, December 4, 2023. https://abcnews.go.com/US/mass-shootings-days-2023-database-shows/story?id=96609874/.

Amuno, Alfred. "Generation Years Chart: 20th to 21st Century Generations." *Parenting Alpha*, November 2, 2022. https://parentingalpha.com/generation-years-chart-20th-to-21st-century-generations/.

Banda, SreeRam. "Events that Shaped the US in the Past Decade (2000–2010)—Part 1 of 3." *International Business Times*, December 29, 2010. https://www.ibtimes.com/events-shaped-us-past-decade-2000-2010-part-1-3-252111.

Barajas, Joshua. "How Trump's Family Separation Policy Became What It Is Today." *PBS NewsHour*, June 21, 2018. https://www.pbs.org/newshour/nation/how-trumps-family-separation-policy-has-become-what-it-is-today.

Barnicoat, Becky, and Nicky Woolf. "Decade Timeline—The Last 10 Years: What Happened When?" *The Guardian*, October 19, 2009. https://www.theguardian.com/world/2009/oct/17/decade-timeline-what-happened-when.

Berkowitz, David. "13 Things to Know about the Alpha Generation: The Newest Generation Has No Purchasing Power Yet, but Will Soon Take Over the World." *Ad Age*, January 28, 2016. https://adage.com/article/digitalnext/13-things-alpha-generation/302366/.

Berryman, Jerome W. *Becoming like a Child: The Curiosity of Maturity beyond the Norm.* New York: Church Publishing, 2017. Kindle.

———. *Children and the Theologians: Clearing the Way for Grace.* New York: Morehouse Publishing, 2009. Kindle.

Blanding, DeShawn, and Danyelle Solomon. "The Coronavirus Pandemic Is Fueling Fear and Hate across America." Center for American Progress, March 30, 2020. https://

Bibliography

www.americanprogress.org/issues/race/news/2020/03/30/482407/coronavirus-pandemic-fueling-fear-hate-across-america/.

Blount, Reginald. "From Sabbath Schools to Freedom Schools: Christian Vocation and the Power of Voice." In *Educating for Redemptive Community: Essays in Honor of Jack Seymour and Margaret Ann Crain*, edited by Denise Janssen, 65–77. Eugene, OR: Wipf and Stock, 2015.

Bostock, Bill. "Trump's First Tweet about a 'Chinese Virus' Caused an Increase of Anti-Asian Hashtags on Twitter, Study Finds." *Insider*, March 22, 2021. https://www.businessinsider.com/trump-chinese-virus-tweet-sparked-anti-asian-hashtags-spike-study-2021-3.

Budiman, Abby. "Koreans in the U.S. Fact Sheet." Pew Research Center, April 29, 2021. https://www.pewresearch.org/social-trends/fact-sheet/asian-americans-koreans-in-the-u-s/.

Budiman, Abby, and Neil G. Ruiz. "Key Facts about Asian Americans, a Diverse and Growing Population." Pew Research Center, April 29, 2021. https://www.pewresearch.org/fact-tank/2021/04/29/key-facts-about-asian-americans/.

Bunge, Marcia J. Introduction to *The Child in Christian Thought*, edited by Marcia J. Bunge, 1–28. Grand Rapids: Eerdmans, 2001.

Caldwell, Elizabeth F. *God's Big Table: Nurturing Children in a Diverse World*. Cleveland: Pilgrim, 2011.

———. *I Wonder: Engaging a Child's Curiosity about the Bible*. Nashville: Abingdon, 2016.

———. *Making a Home for Faith: Nurturing the Spiritual Life of Your Children*, rev. ed. Cleveland: Pilgrim, 2007.

———. "Religious Instruction: Homemaking." In *Mapping Christian Education: Approaches to Congregational Learning*, edited by Jack L. Seymour, 74–89. Nashville: Abingdon, 1997.

Campen, Tanya Marie Eustace. *Holy Work with Children: Making Meaning Together*. Eugene, OR: Pickwick, 2021.

Carter, Warren. "The Gospel according to Matthew." In *The New Interpreter's Study Bible: New Revised Standard Version with the Apocrypha*, 1745–1800. Nashville: Abingdon, 2003.

Chavez, Nicole. "Asian Americans Reported Being Targeted at Least 500 Times in the Last Two Months." CNN, March 16, 2021. https://edition.cnn.com/2021/03/16/us/asian-americans-hate-incidents-report/index.html.

Chiu, Allyson. "An All-Asian Cast and No Martial Arts: Why the 'Crazy Rich Asians' Movie Matters." *The Washington Post*, April 26, 2018. https://www.washingtonpost.com/news/morning-mix/wp/2018/04/26/an-all-asian-cast-and-no-martial-arts-why-the-crazy-rich-asians-movie-matters/?noredirect=on.

Choi, Yoonjung, and Jae Hoon Lim. "Korean Newcomer Youth's Experiences of Racial Marginalization and Internalization of the Model Minority Myth." In *Killing the Model Minority Stereotype: Asian American Counterstories and Complicity*, edited by Nicholas D. Hartlep and Bradley J. Porfilio, 165–84. Charlotte, NC: Information Age, 2015.

Chou, Chih-Chieh. "Critique on the Notion of Model Minority: An Alternative Racism to Asian American?" *Asian Ethnicity* 9, no. 3 (October 2008) 219–29.

Chung, Sinai. "Mozying: When the Young Mentor the Younger." In *Greenhouses of Hope: Congregations Growing Young Leaders Who Will Change the World*, edited by Dori Grinenko Baker, 57–82. Herndon, VA: Alban Institute, 2010.

Corey, Dan. "2017 Year in Review: Here Are the Top 10 Biggest News Stories." *NBC News.* December 26, 2017. https://www.nbcnews.com/news/us-news/2017-year-review-here-are-top-10-biggest-news-stories-n828881.

Couture, Pamela D. *Seeing Children, Seeing God: A Practical Theology of Children and Poverty.* Nashville: Abingdon, 2000.

Crain, Margaret Ann. *The United Methodist Deacon: Ordained to Word, Service, Compassion, and Justice.* Nashville: Abingdon, 2014. Kindle.

Crain, Margaret Ann, and Jack L. Seymour. "The Ethnographer as Minister: Ethnographic Research in Ministry." *Religious Education* 91, no. 3 (Summer 1996) 299–315.

Crain, William. *Theories of Development: Concepts and Applications*, 4th ed. Upper Saddle River, NJ: Prentice Hall, 2000.

Cully, Iris V., and Kendig Brubaker Cully, ed. *Harper's Encyclopedia of Religious Education.* San Francisco: Harper & Row, 1990.

Duffin, Erin. "U.S. Population by Generation 2021." *Statista,* October 11, 2022. https://www.statista.com/statistics/797321/us-population-by-generation/.

Elmore, Tim. *Generation Z Unfiltered: Facing Nine Hidden Challenges of the Most Anxious Population.* Atlanta: Poet Gardener, 2019.

Erikson, Erik H. *Childhood and Society.* New York: W. W. Norton, 1993.

Everist, Norma Cook. "Who Is the Child? Whose Is the Child? A Theology of Children." In *The Ministry of Children's Education,* edited by Barbara S. Wilson, Mark Gardner, and James Satter, chap. 3. Minneapolis: Fortress, 2004.

Fong, Timothy P. *The Contemporary Asian American Experience: Beyond the Model Minority.* 3rd ed. Upper Saddle River, NJ: Prentice Hall, 2008.

Fowler, Hayley. "'God Will Protect Me.' Here's How Religious Americans View the Coronavirus Pandemic." *Charlotte Observer,* May 16, 2020. https://www.charlotteobserver.com/news/coronavirus/article242784396.html.

Fowler, James W. "Strength for the Journey: Early Childhood Development in Selfhood and Faith." In *Faith Development in Early Childhood,* edited by Doris A. Blazer, 1–36. Kansas City, MO: Sheed & Ward, 1989.

Freire, Paulo. *Pedagogy of the Oppressed.* 30th anniv. ed. Translated by Myra Bergman Ramos. New York: Bloomsbury, 2012.

Fretheim, Terence E. "'God Was with the Boy' (Genesis 21:20): Children in the Book of Genesis." In *The Child in the Bible,* edited by Marcia J. Bunge, Terence E. Fretheim, and Beverly Roberts Gaventa, chap. 1. Grand Rapids: Eerdmans, 2008. Kindle.

Furnish, Dorothy Jean. *Experiencing the Bible with Children.* Nashville: Abingdon, 1990.

Gardiner, Harry W. *Lives across Cultures: Cross-Cultural Human Development.* 6th ed. New York: Pearson, 2018.

Gardiner, Harry W., and Corinne Kosmitzki. *Lives across Cultures: Cross-Cultural Human Development.* 4th ed. Boston: Allyn and Bacon, 2008.

Giroux, Henry A. *On Critical Pedagogy.* New York: Continuum, 2011.

———. "Rethinking Education as the Practice of Freedom: Paulo Freire and the Promise of Critical Pedagogy," *Policy Futures in Education* 8, no. 6 (2010) 715–21. https://doi.org/10.2304/pfie.2010.8.6.715.

Goto, Courtney T. "Asian American Practical Theologies." In *Opening the Field of Practical Theology: An Introduction,* edited by Kathleen A. Cahalan and Gordon S. Mikoski, chap. 3. Lanham, MD: Rowman & Littlefield, 2014. Kindle.

———. *The Grace of Playing: Pedagogies for Leaning into God's New Creation.* Eugene, OR: Pickwick, 2016.

Bibliography

Grobbelaar, Jan. "Jesus and the Children in the Gospel of Matthew." In *Theologies of Childhood and the Children of Africa*, edited by Jan Grobbelaar and Gert Breed, chap. 5. Durbanville, South Africa: AOSIS, 2006. Kindle.

Groody, Daniel G. "Crossing the Divide: Foundations of a Theology of Migration and Refugees." *Theological Studies* 70, no. 3 (September 2009) 638–67. https://doi.org/10.1177/004056390907000306.

Gruger, William. "PSY's 'Gangnam Style' Video Hits 1 Billion Views, Unprecedented Milestone." *Billboard*. December 21, 2012. https://www.billboard.com/music/music-news/psys-gangnam-style-video-hits-1-billion-views-unprecedented-milestone-1483733/.

Gundry, Judith M. "Children in the Gospel of Mark, with Special Attention to Jesus' Blessing of the Children (Mark 10:13–16) and the Purpose of Mark." In *The Child in the Bible*, edited by Marcia J. Bunge, Terence E. Fretheim, and Beverly Roberts Gaventa, chap. 7. Grand Rapids: Eerdmans, 2008. Kindle.

Gundry-Volf, Judith M. "The Least and the Greatest: Children in the New Testament." In *The Child in Christian Thought*, edited by Marcia J. Bunge, 29–60. Grand Rapids: Eerdmans, 2001.

Hamman, Jaco. "Playing." In *The Wiley Blackwell Companion to Practical Theology*, edited by Bonnie J. Miller-McLemore. 42–50. Malden, MA: Wiley Blackwell, 2014.

Han, Arar, and John Y. Hsu. Introduction to *Asian American X: An Intersection of 21st Century Asian American Voices*, edited by Arar Han and John Hsu, 1–14. Ann Arbor: University of Michigan Press, 2004.

Harris, Maria. *Fashion Me a People: Curriculum in the Church*. Louisville: Westminster John Knox, 1989.

Hartlep, Nicholas D., and Antonio L. Ellis. "The 'Model Minority' Myth: A Critical Race Theoretical Analysis of Asian Americans in America's Most Segregated City." In *Killing the Model Minority Stereotype: Asian American Counterstories and Complicity*, edited by Nicholas D. Hartlep and Bradley J. Porfilio, 335–55. Charlotte, NC: Information Age, 2015.

Hegarty, Aaron. "Timeline: Immigrant Children Separated from Families at the Border." *USA Today*, July 25, 2018. https://www.usatoday.com/story/news/2018/06/27/immigrant-children-family-separation-border-timeline/734014002/.

Helsel, Phil, and Rachael Elbaum. "8 Dead in Atlanta-Area Spa Shootings, Suspect Arrested." *NBC News*, March 17, 2021. https://www.nbcnews.com/news/us-news/3-dead-shooting-georgia-massage-parlor-suspect-loose-n1261262.

Hertig, Young Lee. *Cultural Tug of War: The Korean Immigrant Family and Church in Transition*. Nashville: Abingdon, 2001.

Hill, Evan, Ainara Tiefenthaler, Christiaan Triebert, Drew Jordan, Haley Willis, and Robin Stein. "How George Floyd Was Killed in Police Custody." *New York Times*, March 18, 2021. https://www.nytimes.com/2020/05/31/us/george-floyd-investigation.html.

Ho, Karen K. "*Crazy Rich Asians* Is Going to Change Hollywood. It's About Time." *Time*, August 15, 2018. http://time.com/longform/crazy-rich-asians/.

Hong, Cathy Park. *Minor Feelings: An Asian American Reckoning*. New York: Random House, 2020.

hooks, bell. *Teaching to Transgress: Education as the Practice of Freedom*. New York: Routledge, 1994.

Hwang, Heesung. "Encounter with Sewol: Madang as a Possibility of Interreligious Solidarity for Social Justice in South Korea." *REA Annual Meeting 2017 Proceedings*,

477–88. Religious Education Association, 2017. https://religiouseducation.net/papers/proceedings-REA2017.pdf.

———. "Korean Churches Must Nurture Younger Generations." *UM News*, May 26, 2021. https://www.umnews.org/en/news/korean-churches-must-nurture-younger-generations.

Hyun, Eunsook. *Making Sense of Developmentally and Culturally Appropriate Practice (DCAP) in Early Childhood Education*. New York: Peter Lang, 1998.

Iovino, Joe. "Disciples Making Disciples: Life-Transforming Small Groups." United Methodist Church, August 10, 2015. http://www.umc.org/what-we-believe/disciples-making-disciples-life-transforming-small-groups.

Jeffrey, Courtland. "Mass Shootings in the U.S.: When, Where They Have Occurred in 2018." *ABC15 Arizona*, November 8, 2018. https://www.abc15.com/news/data/mass-shootings-in-the-us-when-where-they-have-occurred-in-2018.

Jensen, David H. *Graced Vulnerability: A Theology of Childhood*. Cleveland: Pilgrim, 2005.

Jeung, Russell, Carolyn Chen, and Jerry Z. Park. "Introduction: Religious, Racial, and Ethnic Identities of the New Second Generation." In *Sustaining Faith Traditions: Race, Ethnicity, and Religion among the Latino and Asian American Second Generation*, edited by Carolyn Chen and Russell Jeung, 1–24. New York: New York University Press, 2012.

Jin, Dal Young. *New Korean Wave: Transnational Cultural Power in the Age of Social Media*. Chicago: University of Illinois Press, 2016. Kindle.

Jones, Robert P. *The End of White Christian America*. New York: Simon & Schuster, 2016.

Kang, Steve S. "Reflections upon Methodology: Research on Themes of Self Construction and Self Integration in the Narrative of Second Generation Korean American Young Adults." *Religious Education* 96, no. 3 (Summer 2001) 408–15.

Kawai, Yuko. "Stereotyping Asian Americans: The Dialectic of the Model Minority and the Yellow Peril." *Harvard Journal of Communications* 16 (2005) 109–30.

Kibria, Nazli. *Becoming Asian American: Second-Generation Chinese and Korean American Identities*. Baltimore: Johns Hopkins University Press, 2002.

Kids Count Data Center. "Child Population by Race and Ethnicity in the United States, 2012–2021." *Annie E. Casey Foundation*, October 2022. https://datacenter.kidscount.org/data/tables/103-child-population-by-race-and-ethnicity#detailed/1/any/false/2048,574,1729,37,871,870,573,869,36,868/68,69,67,12,70,66,71,72/423,424.

Kim, Grace Ji-Sun. *Embracing the Other: The Transformative Spirit of Love*. Grand Rapids: Eerdmans, 2015.

———. *Invisible: Theology and the Experience of Asian American Women*. Minneapolis: Fortress, 2021.

———. *Madang*. Apple Podcasts. https://podcasts.apple.com/us/podcast/madang/id1556774235.

Kim, Grace Sangok. "Asian North American Immigrant Parents and Youth: Parenting and Growing Up in a Cultural Gap." In *People on the Way: Asian North Americans Discovering Christ, Culture, and Community*, edited by David Ng, 129–45. Valley Forge, PA: Judson, 1996.

Kim, Ilpyong J. "A Century of Korean Immigration to the United States: 1903–2003." In *Korean-Americans: Past, Present, and Future*, edited by Ilpyong J. Kim, 13–37. Elizabeth, NJ: Hollym International, 2004.

Kim, Jean. "Asian American Identity Development Theory." In *New Perspectives on Racial Identity Development: A Theoretical and Practical Anthology*, edited by Charmaine

Bibliography

L. Wijeyesinghe and Bailey W. Jackson III, 67–90. New York: New York University Press, 2001.

Kim, Jung Ha. *Bridge-Makers and Cross-Bearers: Korean-American Women and the Church.* Atlanta: Scholars, 1997.

Kim, Sara Cho. "A Model Minority in Distress: Threats to Korean American Undergraduates' Identity and Well-Being." PhD diss., University of Wisconsin-Madison, 2009.

Kim, Sharon. *A Faith of Our Own: Second-Generation Spirituality in Korean American Churches.* New Brunswick: Rutgers University Press, 2010.

Kim, Sharon, and Rebecca Y. Kim. "Second-Generation Korean American Christians' Communities: Congregational Hybridity." In *Sustaining Faith Traditions: Race, Ethnicity, and Religion among the Latino and Asian American Second Generation*, edited by Carolyn Chen and Russell Jeung, 176–93. New York: New York University Press, 2012.

Kim-Cragg, HyeRan. *Interdependence: A Postcolonial Feminist Practical Theology.* Eugene, OR: Pickwick, 2018. Kindle.

Klappenecker, Gabriele. "The Development of Public Responsibility in James William Fowler's Theology and Psychology." In *Developing a Public Faith: New Directions in Practical Theology*, edited by Richard R. Osmer and Friedrich L. Schweitzer, 43–59. St. Louis: Chalice, 2003.

Lee, Dae Kyun. "마당, 아직 잃어버리지 않았다" [Madang, we have not lost it yet]. *The Architecture Review Blog* 마당 [Madang]. December 26, 2015. http://madangsr.tistory.com/90.

Lee, Jennifer, and Min Zhou. *The Asian American Achievement Paradox.* New York: Russell Sage Foundation, 2015.

Lee, Jung Young. *Marginality: The Key to Multicultural Theology.* Minneapolis: Fortress, 1995.

Lee, Stacey J. *Unraveling the "Model Minority" Stereotype: Listening to Asian American Youth.* 2nd ed. New York: Teachers College Press, 2009.

Lynch, Joe. "BTS Brings 'DNA' and Flashy Choreography to 2017 AMAs." *Billboard*, November 19, 2017. https://www.billboard.com/articles/events/amas/8039540/bts-dna-amas-2017.

Lynch, Sarah N., and Valerie Volcovici. "Atlanta Shooting of Asian Women Was Racially Motivated, U.S. Senator Says." *Reuters*, March 21, 2021. https://www.reuters.com/article/us-crime-georgia-spas/atlanta-shooting-of-asian-women-was-racially-motivated-u-s-senator-says-idUSKBN2BD0LW.

Mercer, Joyce Ann. *Welcoming Children: A Practical Theology of Childhood.* St. Louis: Chalice, 2005.

Miller-McLemore, Bonnie J. *In the Midst of Chaos: Caring for Children as Spiritual Practice.* San Francisco: John Wiley & Sons, 2007.

———. *Let the Children Come: Reimagining Childhood from a Christian Perspective.* San Francisco: Jossey-Bass, 2003.

Montero, M. Kristiina. "Standing #WithRefugees," review of *Supporting Refugee Children: Strategies for Educators*, by Jan Stewart. *Journal of Adolescent and Adult Literacy* 62, no. 1 (July/August 2018) 123–25. https://doi.org/10.1002/jaal.866.

Mooney, Carol Garhart. *Theories of Childhood: An Introduction to Dewey, Montessori, Erikson, Piaget, and Vygotsky.* 2nd ed. St. Paul: Redleaf, 2013.

Bibliography

Moore, Mary Elizabeth. "Foreword: A Gift of Redemptive Love." In *Educating for Redemptive Community: Essays in Honor of Jack Seymour and Margaret Ann Crain*, edited by Denise Janssen, xi–xvii. Eugene, OR: Wipf & Stock, 2015.
Neal, Cynthia Jones. "The Power of Vygotsky." In *Nurture That Is Christian: Developmental Perspectives on Christian Education*, edited by James C. Wilhoit and John M. Dettoni, 123–38. Grand Rapids: Baker Books, 1995.
Ng, Greer Anne Wenh-In. "Asian North American Youth: A Ministry of Self-Identity and Pastoral Care." In *People on the Way: Asian North Americans Discovering Christ, Culture, and Community*, edited by David Ng, 201–27. Valley Forge, PA: Judson, 1996.
———. "Beyond Bible Stories: The Role of Culture-Specific Myths/Stories in the Identity Formation of Nondominant Immigrant Children." *Religious Education* 99, no. 2 (Spring 2004) 125–36.
———. "Family and Education from an Asian North-American Perspective: Implications for the Church's Educational Ministry." *Religious Education* 87, no. 1 (Winter 1992) 52–61.
———. "From Confucian Master Teacher to Freirean Mutual Learner: Challenges in Pedagogical Practice and Religious Education." *Religious Education* 95, no. 3 (Summer 2000) 308–19.
Ng, Jennifer C., Sharon S. Lee, and Yoon K. Pak. "Contesting the Model Minority and Perpetual Foreigner Stereotypes: A Critical Review of Literature on Asian Americans in Education." *Review of Research in Education* 31 (March 2007) 95–130. http://www.jstor.org/stable/20185103.
OECD. *Trends Shaping Education 2016*. Paris: OECD Publishing, 2016. http://dx.doi.org/10.1787/trends_edu-2016-en.
Omi, Michael, and Howard Winant. *Racial Formation in the United States: From the 1960s to the 1990s*. 2nd ed. New York: Routledge, 1994.
O'Neill, Brian. "Ecological Perspectives and Children's Use of the Internet: Exploring Micro to Macro Level Analysis." *Estonian Journal of Education* 3, no. 2 (2015) 32–53.
Otoshi, Kathryn. *One*. Novato, CA: KO Kids, 2008.
Paik, Susan J. "Introduction, Background, and International Perspectives: Korean History, Culture, and Education." *International Journal of Educational Research* 35, no. 6 (2001) 535–607.
Park, Linda Sue. *Bee-Bim Bop!* New York: Clarion, 2005.
Park, Lisa Sun-Hee. "Continuing Significance of the Model Minority Myth: The Second Generation." In *Contemporary Asian America: A Multidisciplinary Reader*, 3rd ed., edited by Min Zhou and Anthony C. Ocampo, 497–507. New York: New York University Press, 2016.
Parks, Brad. "George Floyd's Death Was 'Murder' and the Accused Officer 'Knew What He Was Doing,' Minneapolis Police Chief Says." CNN, June 24, 2020. https://www.cnn.com/2020/06/24/us/minneapolis-police-chief-comment-george-floyd-trnd/index.html.
Parks, Sharon Daloz. *Big Questions, Worthy Dreams: Mentoring Emerging Adults in Their Search for Meaning, Purpose, and Faith*. 2nd ed. San Francisco: Jossey-Bass, 2011.
Portes, Alejandro, and Rubén G. Rumbaut. *Immigrant America: A Portrait*. 4th ed. Oakland, CA: University of California Press, 2014.
Rishi, Sunny. "Education Fever and Its Impact on South Korea." Accessed December 3, 2022. https://paperzz.com/doc/9185857/education-fever-and-its-impact-on-south-korea.

Bibliography

Rodriguez, Joe Fitzgerald, and Holly McDede. "Report: Asian Americans More Stressed by Anti-Asian Hate Than COVID-19." KQED, June 1, 2021. https://www.kqed.org/news/11876061/report-asian-americas-more-stressed-by-anti-asian-hate-than-covid-19.

Ruether, Rosemary Radford. "Christian Quest for Redemptive Community." *CrossCurrents* 38, no. 1 (Spring 1988) 3–16.

Sergent, Jim. "Boulder Grocery Store Rampage Follows Spike in Mass Shootings During 2020." *USA Today*, March 24, 2021. https://www.usatoday.com/in-depth/news/2021/03/23/boulder-shooting-follows-spike-gun-violence-during-2020/6965360002/.

Serjeant, Jill. "A Year After 'Parasite,' Korean-Language Movie 'Minari' Is Talk of Hollywood." *Reuters*, February 17, 2021. https://www.reuters.com/article/us-film-minari/a-year-after-parasite-korean-language-movie-minari-is-talk-of-hollywood-idUSKBN2AH1UW.

Seymour, Jack L. "Approaches to Christian Education." In *Mapping Christian Education: Approaches to Congregational Learning*, edited by Jack L. Seymour, 9–22. Nashville: Abingdon, 1997.

———. "Pay Attention: Educating for Redemptive Communities." In *Educating for Redemptive Community: Essays in Honor of Jack Seymour and Margaret Ann Crain*, edited by Denise Janssen, 10–28. Eugene, OR: Wipf and Stock, 2015.

———. *Teaching Biblical Faith: Leading Small Group Bible Studies*. Nashville: Abingdon, 2015.

———. *Teaching the Way of Jesus: Educating Christians for Faithful Living*. Nashville: Abingdon, 2014.

———. 예수님이 직접 가르쳐준 교육학 [Teaching the way of Jesus]. Translated by SungJoo Oh. Seoul: Shinang & Jisung, 2015.

Seymour, Jack L., Margaret Ann Crain, and Joseph V. Crockett. *Educating Christians: The Intersection of Meaning, Learning, and Vocation*. Nashville: Abingdon, 1993.

Shin, Sarah. *Beyond Colorblind: Redeeming Our Ethnic Journey*. Downers Grove, IL: IVP, 2017.

Silverstein, Jason. "There Were More Mass Shootings Than Days in 2019." CBS News, January 2, 2020. https://www.cbsnews.com/news/mass-shootings-2019-more-than-days-365/.

Slotkin, Richard. *Regeneration through Violence: The Mythology of the American Frontier, 1600–1860*. Norman: University of Oklahoma Press, 1973.

Smith, Robert London, Jr. *From Strength to Strength: Shaping a Black Practical Theology for the 21st Century*. New York: Peter Lang, 2007.

Smith, Yolanda Y. *Reclaiming the Spirituals: New Possibilities for African American Christian Education*. Cleveland: Pilgrim, 2004.

Spring, Joel. *Wheels in the Head: Educational Philosophies of Authority, Freedom, and Culture from Socrates to Paulo Freire*. New York: McGraw-Hill, 1994.

Sterbenz, Christina. "Here's Who Comes After Generation Z—and They'll Be the Most Transformative Age Group Ever." *Insider*, December 5, 2015. https://www.businessinsider.com/generation-alpha-2014-7-2?r=UK&IR=T.

Sterling, Greg. "Move Over Millennials, Gen-Z Now the Largest Single Population Segment." *MarTech*, July 17, 2017. https://marketingland.com/move-millennials-gen-z-now-largest-single-population-segment-219788.

Stevens, Ellen. "We Are Family: Thoughts on the Kin-dom of God." *Feminist Theology* 2 (blog). Seattle School of Theology and Psychology, March 22, 2016. https://

medium.com/feminist-theology-2/we-are-family-views-on-the-kin-dom-of-god-fc63cc3b1a6a.

Stewart, Jan. *Supporting Refugee Children: Strategies for Educators.* North York, ON: University of Toronto Press, 2011.

Sue, Stanley, and Harry H. L. Kitano. "Stereotypes as a Measure of Success." *Journal of Social Issues* 29, no. 2 (1973) 83–98.

Tse, Justin. "The 'Suffering' of the Model Minority (My Conversion to Liberal Theology #10)." *Eastern Catholic Person* (blog). *Patheos*, December 22, 2017. http://www.patheos.com/blogs/ecperson/2017/12/22/suffering-model-minority-conversion-liberation-theology-10/.

Ty, Eleanor. *Asianfail: Narratives of Disenchantment and the Model Minority.* Urbana: University of Illinois Press, 2017.

UMC Peace Initiative. 함께 이루어가는 하나님 나라 [The Kin-dom of God we build together]. Seoul: Sinang & Jisung, 2021.

United Nations, Department of Economic and Social Affairs, Population Division. *World Population Ageing, 2015.* New York: United Nations, 2015.

Van Gorder, Andrew Christian. "Pedagogy for the Children of the Oppressors: Liberative Education for Social Justice among the World's Privileged." *Journal of Transformative Education* 5, no. 1 (January 2007) 8–32.

Vmiller373. "2000–2010 Major Events." Timetoast Timelines. Accessed November 28, 2022. https://www.timetoast.com/timelines/2000-2010-major-events.

Vygotsky, Lev S. *Mind in Society: The Development of Higher Psychological Processes.* Edited by Michael Cole, Vera John-Steiner, Sylvia Scribner, and Ellen Souberman. Cambridge: Harvard University Press, 1978.

West, Nathaniel. "Religious Educators as Public Ministry Leaders." In *From Lament to Advocacy: Black Religious Education and Public Ministry*, edited by Anne E. Streaty Wimberly, Nathaniel D. West, and Annie Lockhart-Gilroy, 31–58. Nashville: Wesley's Foundery, 2020.

Westerhoff, John H., III. *Will Our Children Have Faith?* 3rd revised ed. New York: Morehouse, 2012. Kindle.

White, James Emery. *Meet Generation Z: Understanding and Reaching the New Post-Christian World.* Grand Rapids, MI: Baker, 2017.

White, Keith J. "'He Placed a Little Child in the Midst': Jesus, the Kingdom, and Children." In *The Child in the Bible*, edited by Marcia J. Bunge, Terence E. Fretheim, and Beverly Roberts Gaventa, chap.16. Grand Rapids: Eerdmans, 2008. Kindle.

Wimberly, Anne E. Streaty. *Soul Stories: African American Christian Education.* Rev. ed. Nashville: Abingdon, 2005.

Yoo, Hyun Joon. "아파트에 살면서도 '집집마다 앞마당' 누리며 살 수 있다면" [You can enjoy your own front madang while living in an apartment]. *Hani*, August 21, 2021. www.hani.co.kr/arti/culture/culture_general/1008569.html.

Yust, Karen-Marie. *Real Kids, Real Faith: Practices for Nurturing Children's Spiritual Lives.* San Francisco: Jossey-Bass, 2004.

Zhou, Li. "The Long History of Anti-Asian Hate in America, Explained." *Vox*, March 5, 2021. https://www.vox.com/identities/2020/4/21/21221007/anti-asian-racism-coronavirus-xenophobia.

Zhou, Min. "Growing Up American: The Challenge Confronting Immigrant Children and Children of Immigrants." *Annual Reviews: Sociology* 23 (1997) 63–95.

BIBLIOGRAPHY

Zhou, Min, and Carl L. Bankston III. *The Rise of the New Second Generation*. Cambridge: Polity, 2016. Kindle.

Zhou, Min, and Susan S. Kim. "Community Forces, Social Capital, and Educational Achievement: The Case of Supplementary Education in the Chinese and Korean Immigrant Communities." *Harvard Educational Review* 76, no. 1 (Spring 2006) 1–29.

www.ingramcontent.com/pod-product-compliance
Lightning Source LLC
Chambersburg PA
CBHW071450160426
43195CB00013B/2075